I, Pierre Seel, Deported Homosexual

I, Pierre Seel, Deported Homosexual

A MEMOIR OF NAZI TERROR

Pierre Seel

Translated from the French by Joachim Neugroschel

BASIC BOOKS
A Member of the Perseus Books Group
New York

Original French text published as *Moi, Pierre Seel, déporté homosexuel*
Copyright ©1994 by Calmann-Lévy

Books published by Basic Books are available at special discounts for bulk
purchases in the United States by corporations, institutions, and other organizations. For more information, please contact the Special Markets Department at the
Perseus Books Group, 2300 Chestnut Street, Suite 200, Philadelphia, PA 19103,
or call (800) 810-4145, ext. 5000, or e-mail special.markets@perseusbooks.com.

Designed by Elliott Beard

Library of Congress Cataloging-in-Publication Data
Seel, Pierre, 1923–
  [Moi, Pierre Seel, déporté homosexuel. English]
  I, Pierre Seel, deported homosexual : a memoir of Nazi Terror / Pierre Seel in
collaboration with Jean Le Bitoux ; translated from the French by Joachim
Neugroschel.
      p.   cm.
  Includes bibliographical references.
  ISBN 0-465-04500-6
  1. Seel, Pierre, 1923–   . 2. Gay men—France—Mulhouse—Biography.
3. Gays—Nazi persecution—France—Mulhouse. 4. World War, 1939–1945—
Deportations from France. 5. World War, 1939–1945—Prisoners and prisons,
French. 6. National socialism. 7. Concentration camps—Germany. I. LeBitoux,
Jean. II. Title.
HQ75.8.S44A3 1995
305.38'9664'092—dc20
[b]   95—12678
                         CIP

Paperback ISBN 978-0-465-01848-2

To my friend Jo
Murdered in 1941
And to all the victims
Of the Nazi barbarity

For one pleasure a thousand pains

François Villon, 1463

Contents

Contents

Foreword
by Gregory Woods

On Remembrance Sunday in November 1977, I took part in a small ceremony to lay a pink-triangle wreath on the war memorial in Norwich, England. I was a doctoral student at the University of East Anglia on the edge of the city, writing my thesis on gay literature. We members of the student gay group had persuaded the students' union to pay for and lay the wreath, in memory of the many men killed by the Nazis for being homosexual.

The announcement of our plans had caused controversy in the local press—ostensibly because the nation's war memorials and the traditions of Remembrance Sunday (on which the United Kingdom formally celebrates the anniversary of Armistice Day, 1918, which brought the First World War to an end) were intended to commemorate British victims of recent wars, not German and other European non-combatants. But there was, we judged, also a homophobic edge in the response to the announcement of our plans. The British Legion, which presides over the formal events of national commemoration, would not allow us to take part in the morning wreath-layings and two-minute silence; so we would lay our pink triangle in the quiet of the afternoon.

Later that day, we were confronted by a small group of hostile protesters. There was no overtly physical threat, but a lot of shouting and finger-pointing. They accused us of being unpatriotic. We accused them of being homophobic— but this word was newly coined, and they had no idea what we meant.

When the president of the students' union went to lay our wreath, a protester snatched it from his hands and tried to hurl it down into the marketplace below the memorial, but it hit the railings and fell to the ground. The angry group shouted at us for several minutes and then abruptly left the scene. We handed the slightly battered wreath to the president, and he placed it on the memorial.

Some time later, two uniformed members of the British Legion removed the wreath and carried it off to their car. We intercepted them and, after a long but quite good-natured argument, they handed it back to us. Once again, we put it back on the memorial. But by the evening it had vanished.

There was nothing especially imaginative, innovative, or daring about the political gesture we had taken part in. Since we were not an especially radical group, we were simply copying what we had heard that other groups had done at any of the universities in London—perhaps where gay liberationists could guarantee themselves a decent crowd when organizing such demonstrations. The so-called "gay holocaust" was one of the themes of the time, as academic historians were piecing together and making sense of the facts of the matter. As an event or series of events, it stood for the extremes to which the oppression of homosexuals might be taken. It merited George Weinberg's newly minted term "homophobia." The gay liberation movement had adopted the pink triangle—as forced on many homosexual internees in the Nazi concentration camps—as one of its symbols. We wore it on lapel badges; it often graced the mastheads of our newspapers; we carried it on banners during our demonstrations.

One of the characteristics of the broad discussion of this theme was an escalation, without evidence, of the estimated numbers of homosexual victims of Nazism (a hundred thousand, a quarter of a million, half a million . . .), and a careless tendency to assume that the Nazis had prosecuted the same kind of campaign against homosexual men as they had against Jews, with the aim of total annihilation as a "final solution" to the homosexual "problem." My feeling now is that such exaggerations were understandable and perhaps inevitable, given that most of us were hearing of the Nazi mistreatment of homosexual men for the first time and that few substantiating facts seemed to be available. Above all, in contrast to the Shoah—the Holocaust of the Jews—this smaller catastrophe had apparently not been furnished with the narrative evidence of survivors. Jewish memoirs of survival had been coming into print ever since the war had ended. Where were the homosexual equivalents?

For lack of firsthand accounts, some writers began to try to build narratives of the homosexual experience under Nazism around fictional characters. The gay holocaust became one of the concerns of the British theatre group Gay Sweatshop. They addressed it in two plays, *As Time Goes By* by Noel Greig and Drew Griffiths (1977), and *Bent* by Martin Sherman (1979). The first of these has successive historical settings, in three main locations: London in the 1890s, Berlin in the 1930s, and New York City in 1969. The aim was to compare and contrast the effects historical circumstances have on gay subcultures and on individual gay men. In each case, police action against gay men leads to drastic outcomes: the London characters decide they must go into exile; the Berlin characters are caught between exile and the horrors, as yet unrealized, of the concentration camps; and the New York characters respond to a police raid on the Stonewall Inn by kicking off a riot, thereby giving spectacular impetus to the gay liberation movement.

In the manner of all of Gay Sweatshop's plays—performances which were always followed by lively discussions with the audience—*As Time Goes By* is agitprop drama with a clear political message, an argument against quietism and the closet. The characters who meet oppression with optimistic discretion, keeping their heads down and hoping for the best, tend not to do well from it: for their invisibility is no more acceptable to the authorities than the flamboyance of the drag queen—and is hardly more secure. The argument is in favor of visibility, pride, and active resistance. The play recognizes that this may have been virtually impossible, except to a few extraordinary individuals, in 1890s London and 1930s Berlin (where the pioneering sexologist Magnus Hirschfeld is one of its characters); but in gay-liberationist New York—and, by implication, in the England in which the play was to be performed—there was no excuse for inaction or for staying in the closet.

On the use of Nazism as the context for the play's central section, Philip Osment, a playwright and director who worked with Gay Sweatshop, later wrote:

Even in 1977 there was a widely held belief that homosexuality had been somehow responsible for the Third Reich. The perverted brutality of that regime was often embodied in plays and films by the queer Brownshirt or SS guard. I remember friends who couldn't understand why Gay Sweatshop was doing a play about Nazi Germany asking, "Weren't most of the Nazis gay anyway?" The fact that homosexuals were sent to the concentration camps was still not widely known and we were often left out when victims of the Holocaust were listed.[1]

The post-war situation of German gay men and lesbians had been exacerbated by a homophobic mythology that had been built up by the propagandists of the anti-Nazi movement. The Nazis were themselves said to be homosexual perverts: hence the imagery of the Hitler Youth; hence also the tailored uniforms and jackboots. This has proved to be one of the most enduring of the myths about Nazism, all the more solidly endorsed whenever yet another biography of Hitler repeats unsubstantiated suggestions either that he was actively homosexual himself or at least that, by reason of poverty, he worked as a rent boy during his youth in Vienna. The need to prove the sexual perversion of Nazism as an ideology, and of its leaders (most of whom were, of course, conventionally heterosexual) as a psychological type, has clouded the clarity of the regime's anti-homosexual vigor.

While *As Time Goes By* was in development, the playwright Martin Sherman, himself both Jewish and gay, had been called in to rehearsals to help the actors with their American accents for its third section. This experience then gave him the idea for a play entirely focused on Germany in the 1930s. Sherman's *Bent* is a play I now find almost unreadably sensationalist. Most of its debates look inspired by gay politics of the 1970s rather than by the catastrophe for homosexual Germans in the 1930s. One of its central themes is the necessity to come out—even in a Nazi concentration camp. The character Horst, who wears the pink

triangle, is at pains to persuade Max, who wears the yellow
star as a Jew, to affirm his gay identity with pride. And, indeed, Max does so after Horst's death, by swapping jackets
with his corpse.[2]

Another of the play's undercurrents, somewhat along the
same lines as Larry Kramer's controversial 1978 novel
Faggots, is an argument against promiscuity and sado-
masochism. For instance, in the penultimate scene of the
second act, as the play is reaching its inevitably fatal climax,
Horst says to Max: "You're like them. You're like the
guards. You're like the Gestapo. We [in the homosexual
subculture of Berlin] stopped being gentle. I watched it,
when we were on the outside. People made pain and called
it love. I don't want to be like that. You don't make love to
hurt." This is so preachily aimed at the play's late-1970s
gay audiences that, for me, it is an infuriating distraction
from the play's far more serious theme. The distracting
comparison of consenting sadomasochists with Gestapo
torturers and murderers severely compromises the play's
otherwise clear, anti-homophobic message.[3]

However, one of the clearly beneficial effects of both *As
Time Goes By* and *Bent* was to show their younger audiences that, even in the worst of times, it was possible—
and necessary—for homosexual men to lead active social
and sexual lives. It is not possible retrospectively to gather
statistics on such matters, but it is worth remembering,
about the 1930s and 1940s, that not all homosexual men

suppressed their desires and either got married or remained celibate; not all who chose to remain unmarried ended up, at best, in solitude, or, at worst, committing suicide. Appalling social circumstances did not always end in tragedy—or even in unhappiness.

The more one studies the history of gay people's lives, the more one is heartened by the evidence that, even in the least likely circumstances, it was possible for love—or for the choice of promiscuous sexual enjoyment—to flourish. Gad Beck, who lived in Nazi Berlin as both a Jew and a gay man, later wrote: "I never felt like an outsider because of my homosexuality. We were all united by a strong sense of solidarity. We were repressed and persecuted, and we had no desire to become people who discriminated against others."[4] These three sentences convey a vivid impression of compensatory subcultural warmth. In this respect, perhaps, oppressed homosexuality is somewhat comparable to poverty. Observing it from more privileged circumstances, it is often difficult to see how people could have survived; but survive they did, and thrive they often did. It is one of the miracles of the human spirit.

Even while still a schoolboy, Pierre Seel had no difficulty finding other men and boys of his own sort and of establishing sexual contact with them, and he knew the risks. Judging by Seel's account, there was little by way of a "gay scene" in his home town of Mulhouse, and none of these was free of risk. There was cruising in Steinbach Square, as well as in other, unnamed public places. There was a room above a café concert where men gathered in the afternoons and where, once its door had been locked, they could have sex together. And there was the balcony of the movie theatre on the Corso.

But if you live outside the law, you cannot then seek help from the agents of the law and trust them to act dispassionately on your behalf. Seel's one great indiscretion was not his association with dubious characters (including the man who stole his watch) but reporting one of them to the police. This was an era of the keeping of lists, and his name was added to one.

Of course, Seel was neither German himself nor living in Germany. But his home region of Alsace, in the Rhinelands, had been for centuries the field of Franco-German disputes. In most recent history, it had been ceded to Germany in 1871 and then returned to France after the First World War in 1919. If Alsace had indeed been, as Seel puts it, "the victim of its geographic location" (p.5), he too would become a victim of that same geography. Once he had appeared on a list compiled by the Alsace police, it was only a matter of time before his name came to the attention of the German authorities.

Nazi policies on homosexuality were, by definition, reactionary. They were vindictive and vengeful, an angry reaction to the perceived excesses of the period of the Weimar Republic, a visible solution to the problem of increased homosexual visibility. In this sense, it might be said that the violent reaction was caused by the progressive gains of the inter-war period: the queers had only themselves to blame. Since then, we have seen the same logic being applied in many countries in response to the spectacular gains of the post-1960s gay rights movement. We see it in the many claims that gay men's deaths in the AIDS epidemic were self-inflicted.

While imprisoning homosexual men as criminals, morally responsible for their crimes against the Reich, the Nazis also used the new discourses of sexology and psychoanalysis, categorising the "condition" of homosexuality as an illness, and giving a spuriously scientific gloss to their attempts to cure it. The language used by their white-coated doctors may have seemed superficially more sympathetic than that of their black-coated Gestapo officers, but the end results were much the same.

I have written in detail elsewhere about how the published memoirs of Rudolf Hoess, the Commandant of Auschwitz, used the language of sexology to express an assumed knowledge of the minds of homosexual men who came into his purview and against whom he committed, ordered, or sanctioned the most repellent atrocities.[5] Hoess looked at such men, to his own satisfaction, with the objective eye of the clinician, determined to eradicate their deviancy with a behavioral or physical cure—by forcing them into sexual intercourse with women, for instance, or by castration—but then applied the same eye, once any individual proved intractable or intransigent, to selecting him for removal from the national body politic. This was the same language of a medicalized sexology that had allowed the individual homosexual man to think himself "born that way" and therefore not immoral because he was unable to "help it." Sexology had defined him, identifying him to himself; but it could also be used against him, identifying him to the authorities.

What was specifically dreadful about the situation of homosexual men and lesbian women in the great whirlwind of hatred that Nazism generated? Many were already living in isolation, unknown to be gay by their families and colleagues at work, perhaps even by their closest friends, and they were often in a depressed state as a consequence of this seclusion. They were indiscriminately regarded as being immoral, criminal, and ill—even by many anti-fascist leftists. Unlike the situation of Jews or gypsies, they had not been brought up by those of their stigmatized own kind— they had not been brought up as gay in gay families, and indeed, if exposed as gay, they often received the most horrified responses from those who were closest to them. Unless firmly ensconced in pockets of queer subculture, they lacked the automatic support that came from being, although an outsider, an insider among outsiders.

The most sobering lesson to be learned from the Nazi abuse of homosexual men is that they did not need to formulate new laws under which to do so; and that, after their defeat, the men who had been imprisoned for homosexual crimes were treated as common criminals by the "liberators" and forced to serve out the full terms of their imprisonment.

Paragraph 175 of the Imperial Penal Code dated from 1871; and, far from being revoked after the defeat of the Nazis, it was strengthened and used more often, not to be liberalized in the East until 1968 and in the West until 1969. Not until decades after the war did Holocaust memorials begin to pay proper attention to the pink triangle internees and deportees; and survivors did not receive compensation. The postwar settlement did not include sympathy for those who were generally agreed to be the dangerous perverts, as the Nazis had condemned them.[6]

As Seel says at the end of Chapter Three, "Liberation was only for others" (p.88). At the end of the war Charles de Gaulle's government extirpated most of the puppet Vichy regime's laws—principally, of course, its various anti-Semitic edicts—but not its anti-homosexual laws, which would not be removed from the statute books until 1981. Homosexual concentration-camp survivors, when they did eventually emerge from imprisonment, tended to have to cover up the nature of the crimes for which they had been incarcerated or deported. They did not emerge as a liberated people; and they had, as yet, no language with which to form common cause and to identify themselves as an oppressed minority. There was no wave of Holocaust memoirs from these men.

After the war, homosexual survivors were still subjected to shame—indeed, in many respects, more so than before the war as the period of peace known as the Cold War began to unfold. Whether they ended up in the East or the "free" West was, in this respect, immaterial. The East regarded homosexuality as a bourgeois perversion with no place in a socialist society; the West regarded it as an untrustworthy psychological condition, leaving one open to entrapment and blackmail by Red spies. The 1950s and 1960s were the heyday of aversive treatments for homosexuality and prosecutions for homosexual acts. This is why the homophile movement of the 1950s and the gay movement that followed it regarded reform of the institutions of mental health as no less crucial and urgent than law reform.

As the gay liberation movement of the 1960s and 1970s developed an interest in the history of the oppression of gay men and lesbians—an interest that soon became manifest in the first wave of publications by academics working in what would come to be called "lesbian and gay studies"[7]— it seemed increasingly urgent to try to collect the memories of previous generations while they could still be heard firsthand. The elderly were witnesses to history, and their voices needed to be heard in their own tone, undistorted by the requirements of the gay movement itself.

But not many such witnesses could be found; and even fewer could be persuaded, after decades of discretion, to speak out. Even the most tactful young gay liberationist could seem threatening to old men who were still scarred by their wartime experiences. This is why Pierre Seel's book is so valuable to historians of institutionalized homophobia.

It has a unique place in the literature of the broader Holocaust, alongside that of the Shoah. As much as it is invaluable in its own right, it also has to stand for all those other memoirs that were never written, either by those men who perished in or on their way to the camps, or by those who served their time and survived the war but then, perforce, returned to the shadows of everyday life in what would come to be called "the closet." Seel's memoir is the type and prototype of others we can only imagine.[8]

When Seel revisits the location of the Schirmeck/ Vorbrüch camp in 1989, he finds it transformed into a residential suburb, with only the cast-iron gates of the camp preserved, decorating the facade of the town hall. A plaque and a sculpture ("hypocritically," he says) are expected to perform the whole task of the commemoration of history. As anyone who has visited a post-1989 east-European sculpture park now hidden away in the suburbs of a Soviet-satellite capital will tell you, there is a limit to the effectiveness of monument-builders' sincere but ultimately bombastic symbolism. One sees the same problem in many of the designs for the post-9/11 rebuilding of the World Trade Center site, including those designs chosen to be realized. Monuments tend to be rather demanding of those who encounter them: they announce emotion, but only rarely can they authentically evoke it. This is where the personal accounts of survivors come in—of Auschwitz or Stalingrad, of the Cultural Revolution or 9/11, of Beslan or Srebrenica.

It is in this context—of the dubious reliability of plaques and sculptures in evoking for new generations particular horrors of the past—that we should think of the memoirs of Holocaust survivors. A monument can, of course, be scanned in a complacent moment or captured in the click of a tourist's camera, whereas a book takes a certain amount of time and effort to be appreciated. A monument can be seen by accident, in passing, whereas the reading of a book takes an initial act of will, followed by a temporary commitment.

But physical memorials remain important, too. In the Netherlands, the Homomonument Foundation was established in 1979, and the Homomonument itself was finally unveiled in Amsterdam in September 1987. It consists of three equilateral triangles of pink marble forming the points of a larger triangle, one of them projecting out onto a canal and pointing towards the National War Memorial on Dam Square. It was not until the 1980s and 1990s that most of the pink-triangle memorial plaques were installed at the concentration-camp sites themselves—all under pressure of the new spirit of gay liberation, sharpened in urgency by the AIDS epidemic: Mauthausen 1984, Dachau 1985, Neuengamme 1985, Sachsenhausen 1992, and so on. The Gay Holocaust Memorial in Berlin was unveiled in May 2008.

Much as the pink triangle had been adopted as a gay liberationist symbol, it then took its place in the fight against AIDS, most notably on the SILENCE=DEATH Project's buttons, posters, and T-shirts. The decision of American playwright and AIDS activist Larry Kramer, as a Jewish gay man, to call his collected AIDS journalism *Reports from the Holocaust* (1989) was consistent with his arguments about both government responsibility for the scale of the emergency and quietist gay men's responsibility for allowing politicians and medics to get away with their negligence. One thinks of this circumstantial connection between Pierre Seel's generation, gay liberationists' revival of interest in its experiences of the Holocaust, and that younger generation's experience of the AIDS epidemic, when Seel points out that the journalist Jean-Pierre Joecker from *Gai Pied* who first interviewed him about his earlier life, subsequently died with AIDS. Seel's editor Jean Le Bitoux eventually suffered the same fate.

There is a lesson to be learned in all this, as much about the future as the past. Advances can be thrown into reverse; optimism can be misplaced. And yet, reverses can themselves be reversed, and the idealism that drives political resistance can restore genuine grounds for an optimism rooted in the possibility of social change. For all the major advances that lesbians and gay men have achieved in the West in recent decades, it can still be difficult, even dangerous, to be openly gay in the school yard, on the streets of the small town, even in certain districts of the big city. And what has come to be called the "gay lifestyle"—as if there were only one such way of living—has remained extremely controversial from certain political, religious, and other subcultural points of view. Resisting the acceptance of homosexuality remains a crucial article of faith on the political right in the United States—and not just on its abundant radical fringe. I say nothing of those nations in which women's liberation has not even begun to take hold, let alone gay liberation—largely as a consequence of fundamentalist readings of the Bible, the Qu'ran, and other religious texts. My point is about the reversibility of our social advances even in those nations where we have made so much progress that we have allowed ourselves to take it for granted. The triumph of repressive National Socialism over all the experimental freedoms of the Weimar Republic tells us this. The vengeful triumphalism of homophobic responses to the AIDS epidemic in the 1980s in the United States and Western Europe tells us again. I keep my copy of Pierre Seel's book on the same shelf as such AIDS memoirs as Paul Monette's *Borrowed Time* and Mark Doty's *Heaven's Coast*.[9]

I still wear my old, battered pink-triangle lapel badge from time to time. In doing so, I identify myself (of course) as gay, but also as a gay liberationist of a particular vintage; and I take the liberty of allying myself with the memory of those on whom the pink triangle was imposed by the National Socialist ideology: those who were killed for being gay, and those who survived into the post-war era to continue being gay, if only in the circumscribed and still oppressed manner that the "liberatory" regimes of Eastern or Western Europe allowed.

Not until 2003 was Pierre Seel officially recognized as a Holocaust victim by the International Organization for Migration; and in 2008 the municipality of Toulouse posthumously renamed a street in his honour (Rue Pierre Seel—Déporté français pour homosexualité—1923–2005). His book continues to inspire people wherever it is read. For instance, the Lahore artist Anwar Saeed illustrated a sequence of erotic drawings of men on the actual pages of *I, Pierre Seel*; these were displayed in the exhibition *Hanging Fire: Contemporary Art from Pakistan* at the Asia Society in New York City (September 2009–January 2010). Saeed said of these images: "Drawing images of love, pleasure, and decadence was the way I went on to relate with the story, which is more about pain, torture and humiliation." This seems an eminently worthwhile trade-off.

So extreme are the events they relate, that memoirs of the Nazi-run deportations and concentration camps often contain moments of breathtaking absurdity, when the language with which we are so familiar in the everyday usage of our own fortunately peaceful lives seems incapable of accommodating the enormity of even simple truths. We seem to have entered a grotesque phantasmagoria coauthored by Lewis Carroll and the Marquis de Sade. There is such a moment in this book when Seel blandly states, "I was not killed" (p.46). It is an extraordinary sentence for anyone to have to say, yet it is crucial to our understanding of his status as a survivor.

Having been forced to fight on the German side in the Wehrmacht, Seel finds himself, in the dying days of the war, trying to make his way home on foot from Russia. After spending the night in a deserted cottage in a forest, he slicks his hair down with some sewing-machine oil and makes a few camp gestures in the mirror (p.73). This is not a scene he dwells on at any length, but it sticks in my mind as an example of how his gayness—by which I mean not just the tendency to respond to other men with the physical signs of desire, but his cultural and social identity as a gay man—has survived a long sequence of hostile, suppressive circumstances, including torture, rape, starvation, and the threat of summary execution. For me, this image of a young queen's rediscovery of himself takes on some of the emblematic force of its fairytale setting. It is as if a willowy yet spirited Red Riding Hood were to come to life again, mockingly self-aware, after being mauled almost to death by the Wolf.

Notes

1. Philip Osment (ed), *Gay Sweatshop: Four Plays and a Company* (London: Methuen, 1989), p.xxxiv.

2. In the present translation of Seel's book, we see a similar imposition of an American concept from the late 1960s in the title of Chapter Five: "Out of the Closet: A Painful Testimony." The original French chapter title consists of only the second of these two phrases.

3. Martin Sherman, *Bent* (London: Amber Lane Press, 1979), p.67. Because the play had an especially controversial reception when it eventually played in Israel, it has continued to have great resonance for Israeli gays. In Eytan Fox's film *The Bubble* (*Ha-Buah*, 2006), the star-crossed lovers Noam, an Israeli, and Ashraf, a Palestinian, attend a staging of the play; in particular, they are shown holding hands in the audience as Horst and Max make love for the first time.

4. Gad Beck, *An Underground Life: Memoirs of a Gay Jew in Nazi Berlin* (Madison, WI: University of Wisconsin Press, 2000), p.56.

5. Gregory Woods, "The Pink Triangle," *A History of Gay Literature: The Male Tradition* (New Haven & London: Yale University Press, 1998), pp.247–256. The memoir in question is Rudolf Hoess, *Commandant of Auschwitz* (London: Phoenix, 2000), originally published in Polish in 1951 and then in German in 1958.

6. In his memoir of survival, *The Men with the Pink Triangle* (*Die Männer mit dem Rosa Winkel*, 1972), p. 114, Heinz Heger writes: "My request for compensation for the years of concentration camp was rejected by our democratic authorities, for as a pink-triangle prisoner, a homosexual, I had been condemned for a criminal offence, even if I'd not

harmed anyone. No restitution is granted to 'criminal' concentration-camp victims."

7. In Britain, the exemplary text of this sort was Jeffrey Weeks's *Coming Out: Homosexual Politics in Britain, from the Nineteenth Century to the Present* (London: Quartet, 1977).

8. The book's endnotes were compiled by Jean Le Bitoux (1948–2010), one of the heroes of the post-1968 French gay movement, perhaps best known as the founder of the gay newspaper *Gai Pied* and, later, the editor of the *Journal du sida* (AIDS journal: he was himself diagnosed HIV-positive in 1986). His engagement with the fate of Seel's generation of gay men resulted in his founding of Le Mémorial de la Déportation Homosexuelle, and he was the author of a book on the topic, *Les Oubliés de la mémoire* (2002). His imprint is everywhere on the text of Seel's memoir—indeed, to such an extent that it would not be doing Seel a disservice if we thought of Le Bitoux as the book's coauthor.

9. Chapter Five of William J. Spurlin's book *Lost Intimacies: Rethinking Homosexuality under National Socialism* (New York: Peter Lang, 2009), "Discursive Traces of Nazi Homophobia in Contemporary Culture" includes a substantial section on the HIV/AIDS epidemic, pp.94–105.

Acknowledgments

First and foremost I must thank Jean Le Bitoux, without whom this book could never have existed. I must also thank him for consulting so many works, which enabled us to verify facts and dates.

During the writing of this book, my memory has been put through a harsh ordeal. These painful episodes could only arouse similar, equally doleful memories among certain readers. Please forgive me, for this book also constitutes an urgent appeal to witnesses and historians. There is a terrible dearth of writing on this subject. I hope I no longer have to be the only person testifying to the Nazi deportation of homosexuals.

My gratitude also goes to the journalists who heard my story and to Irène Meyer and Denis Cordell. I am also grateful to my Alsatian family and to the family that I awkwardly tried to start: I thank them for their patience and understanding. I also thank all the people who have written to me and shown me their support ever since I began testifying over ten years ago.

I, Pierre Seel, Deported Homosexual

Chapter 1
An Average Middle-Class Family

I was seventeen years old, and I knew cruising the square located on the route between my school and my home was risky. A bunch of us would congregate there after classes. To gossip among ourselves. To wait for a stranger to seduce us. That day, in the arms of a thief, I felt my watch sliding off my wrist. I shouted. He had already fled. How could I know that this trivial incident would shake up my life and destroy it?

I was an elegant young man, dressed in the so-called Zazou style. There weren't many of us Zazous in Mulhouse. Our wardrobe was refined rather than rebellious. Our sophisticated ties and our piped vests were hard to find. To dig them up, we had to patronize a tiny number of downtown stores, including the local branch of Mode de Paris, which received these items from the capital every now and then. Our hair had to be very long, slicked down on the skull with Vaseline à la Tino Rossi, then converging in large layered sections at the back of the neck. Here, too, only a few hairdressers knew how to get it right. This style cost a bundle to maintain, but I could afford it. In the streets, the passersby would look, intrigued, or glare at us. Being Zazou also implied a dubious flirtatiousness. One had to follow the fashion.

I was shocked by the theft of my watch, which had great sentimental value for me. It was a gift from my godmother, my mother's sister, who lived in Paris and whom I admired. She had left Alsace because of a forbidden love for a young Protestant man. When their families found out that the young lovers were of different religions, the wedding plans were scrapped. So she had fled far from that inhospitable land. During her rare visits in Alsace, the only person she saw was her younger sister, my mother.

My aunt had given me this watch for my "solemn communion," which had taken place just recently. In our Alsatian Catholic tradition, this is an extremely important ceremony, celebrated at the end of adolescence. Huge tables are covered with the most elegant linen and the heaviest dishes. I had had the finest suit, the finest candle, the finest ribbon. As everyone watched, I experienced that moment in purity, aware that I was leaving childhood, that a responsible adult was blossoming from the religious little boy, and that henceforth I had to maintain the lifelong respect and affection of my near and dear. The guests had come from everywhere, and my father's sisters, who had traveled all the way from the Lower Rhine, made a great impression in the church with their huge Alsatian hair knots.

The youngest of five sons, I was born on August 16, 1923, in the family mansion of Fillate in Haguenau. My parents ran a highly respected patisserie at 46 rue du Sauvage, the main thoroughfare in Mulhouse. In the tearoom, located between two streets leading to the neighboring department stores, the local bourgeoisie indulged its sweet tooth, devouring ice cream, petits-fours, and other goodies. After managing a similar shop in Haguenau, my father bought this one from its owner in 1913, paying for it in monthly installments. My mother, his fiancée, had been manager of a department store—a highly unusual profession for a woman prior to World War I. When they married, she joined my father in running the pastry shop. For decades, she sat behind the cash register in the middle of the shop, with a kind word for each of her customers. We lived in the apartment upstairs.

My parents had met through a priest. Emma Jeanne, my mother, mistrusted chance encounters, for she didn't want to end up like her older sister: seduced, then crushed by the impossibility of a "mixed" marriage. Mother had explained this to her confessor, who then introduced her to a suitable man. It was, by all accounts, a successful marriage.

Their shop prospered only between the end of World War I, 1918, and the crash of 1929; the previous years were terrible. When the war broke out in 1914, the patisserie was requisitioned, and they had to bake bread for the surrounding barracks. My father went off to war, and my mother, with two baby sons, had to endure the intrusion of booted and helmeted German soldiers. They searched the premises, jabbing their bayonets into the mattresses and even into certain wardrobes without bothering to open them. Anyone who might have been hiding there would have been stabbed to death. Rumors had spread, denunciations might have been made. My parents had indeed hidden some patriots. Our religious faith and our devotion to a free and Catholic France were one and the same.

I remember that in my childhood we enjoyed hearing anecdotes about the war—tales that could fill the youngest among us with a sense of pride in being French and Catholic, though confronted with German Protestantism. We heard about the French flag that my family had concealed in the cellar, digging it out in times of despair and softly crooning the *Marseillaise* while overhead the enemy was tramping the streets. We likewise shared my paternal grandmother's fervent memory of her dead husband, an officer who had graduated from the Saint-Cyr military school. At the age of thirty-seven, after founding the Rhine-and-Moselle Insurance Group, he had succumbed to galloping consumption, which was incurable in those days. More than anything, I recall that my brothers and I prayed a great deal to prevent any recurrence of the war, in which Alsace had been the victim of its geographic location: some fathers and uncles in our family had fought on the German side and some on the French.

I can say I had a happy childhood and adolescence. But while I can easily evoke my parents' life with affection and tenderness, my memories of my own life come less spontaneously. For they are painful—as if my later sufferings had erased my childhood happiness, preserving only the anguished moments.

In regard to school, for instance, I remember the time when classmates put some dead birds in my desk. Upon hearing my shriek, the teacher punished me without listening to my excuses. During gym period, every minute was likewise horrible. Skipping rope in front of the others, I got off to a good start, but when I reached the hurdle, I tripped and went sprawling, making a fool of myself. It must have been an entertaining spectacle, for the other kids laughed their heads off. They were all fans of the city's soccer team and talked about nothing else. It was probably only my parents' good name that kept me from becoming the class scapegoat. In any case, those years left me with an early disgust for male violence.

The summer I was ten years old, my family stayed at the Howald Pass, in a huge mansion set amid fir trees. Beautiful promenades encircled a few luxury hotels, where crowned heads would sometimes stay. In the large dining room of this summer resort, a little girl at a nearby table looked at me and smiled. The relentless surveillance by our families, especially at our age, kept us from meeting and getting to know each other. We could communicate only with winks and prolonged smiles.

How could I talk to her? How could I let her know I loved her? Or at least tell her my name? Trying to confess my love, I slipped a pious image under her door every evening: the picture, which was taken from my missal, had my name on the back. This was too much for our incensed mothers, who had to discuss the matter. Their surveillance was joined by my feeling of guilt. The rather harmless situation grew complicated. I was subjected to such a grave sermon about my childishness that it must have confirmed my sense that a little boy should have no spontaneous feelings for a little girl. Who can say whether homosexuality might not develop from repeated incidents like that?

The more I sought gentleness in others, the worse my temper was and remains. I fly off the handle easily, yelling and exasperating other people. One of my worst temper tantrums took place that same year, when I was ten. It involved a shameful object, my father's large war belt from his hitch in the German army. Inscribed on the metal buckle were the words *Gott mit uns*—God with us. Father would sometimes use the belt to punish my brothers and me.

One day, when he again threatened me with that humiliating punishment, I managed to steal the belt and lock myself in the toilet. I refused to come out unless two conditions were met. The first was that the family had to gather outside the locked door—which they did, to my utter amazement. Second, my father had to swear in front of those witnesses that he would never again inflict that horrible strap on me. He agreed. I was the one most stupefied by my boldness. None of my four older brothers had ever gotten our father to surrender like that. It was no doubt because I was the last of his exhausting offspring that my father gave in to my tantrum. The hated object was put away and, later on, discreetly destroyed.

For lunch, the family rigidly split up between three tables. The men's table stood in the center of the room; my father sat at the head, and to his right sat my brother, who was meant to succeed him. Then came the head of staff, and so on through the trainees at the end of the table. My mother officiated at the women's table, with the female employees of the pastry shop. My maternal aunt reined in the agitation at the table reserved for the youngest children and the cook. In the evening, the house was less of a beehive, the tumult of the day subsided. The whole family might occupy a single table. At both lunch and supper, my father was the only one who spoke and asked questions. We held our tongues. This was not in accordance with some rule; it was simply the tangible sign of great collective respect. Nor did I ever hear my mother contradict him in front of anyone else. Likewise he never raised his voice.

Way out of parental earshot, my brothers would show off by talking about girls and how they fooled around with them. But had they dared to broach these subjects outside our bedrooms, they would have been severely chewed out. Like sex and desire, many other aspects of life were unmentionable. And these secrets were well kept.

For instance, my little sister, who was five years my junior, wasn't really my sister. I didn't find out until I was almost eleven. I was happy to have that little girl among all those boys. All I really noticed was that my father was very protective of her. In 1928 her mother, my father's sister, had died of puerperal fever caused by internal bleeding, which doctors didn't know how to treat back then. Her devastated husband was left with a newborn baby. And so my father had offered to bring up the little girl, a living memory of his sister, with his own children. Her father agreed. Later on he remarried and had other children, but in his will he did not forget that child of his first marriage.

Now one day, when we were waiting for our mother to let us into her office, each in turn, with our monthly report card, I noticed that my little sister's card did not have our family name. After lamenting, as usual, my bad marks in arithmetic and praising my good marks in poetry and religion, my mother asked whether something was bothering me. I told her, and she gave me an honest reply. That was how I got the true version of the situation. Josephine, nicknamed Fifine, was still my little sister. She attended the Jeanne d'Arc secondary school and grew up to be a pretty girl with beautiful ringlets around her fine face. But I wondered how many skeletons a family could keep in its closet.

My good marks in religion were consistent with both my faith and the very devout environment I grew up in. At home we said grace at the table. We also prayed every evening. On Catholic holidays the archpriest and a white-haired father shared our meals. In the morning I got up ahead of my schoolmates and, before classes, I attended Mass, which earned me extra points at school. I loved all the ceremony. Those rites and those emotions gave free rein to my poetic imagination.

Nor did my piety ever interfere with my curiosity. I recall quite clearly that as children, my sister and I peered through the keyhole to watch our aunt, who was a nun in Switzerland and visited us once a year: we wanted to find out what was concealed under her veil. We were able to report enthusiastically to our mother that Sister Séraphica had very long, beautiful hair. Needless to say, our impudence earned us a sound thrashing.

Under such conditions, it was not surprising that my early homosexual attractions occurred during Mass, amid the singing, incense, and candles, in those moments of spiritual elevation and religious emotion.

This was not, however, the first time I felt something for a boy. A few summers earlier, I had been my father's only companion on a trip to a spa. There I met the director's son, who must have been around my age; together we built a cabin of branches and leaves in the heart of the surrounding park. Sheltered from snooping eyes, we enjoyed spending time there. I remember nothing else, but I do know that those were the beginnings of my future homosexuality. Likewise I must have been twelve or thirteen when one day, in Dieppe, I was deeply ruffled, strangely upset, by the sight of naked young men running and playing on the beach. I was not observed by my brothers, who must have been out hunting for a summer romance with girls.

Didn't all this indicate that I already liked men? When did it finally hit me that I was homosexual? No doubt with those incidents and others that I've forgotten. Young as I was, I realized that this difference would create an unbridgeable gap between me and my family.

At fifteen, I was perplexed by the question of how to live like that and what was to become of me. It took me a long time to accept what I was and to admit it. I tried hard to open up to my confessor, only to suffer the consequences of my audacity. When I confessed merely that I had masturbated, the priest refused to give me absolution. For nights on end I suffered the shame of my sin and was haunted by agonizing thoughts of hell. Egged on by my adolescent embarrassment, the priest pursued his investigations, whereby the issue of homosexual desire emerged quite naturally. He probed my conscience with the voyeurism of a hidden camera. His provocative questions inflamed my imagination and stoked my anxieties. Did you do this? Did you want to? Whom with? How? Where? When? How often? Did you feel shame or pleasure? By the time the harassment stopped, I was convinced I was a monster.

For a long time I was caught in a cycle of confession and communion, with absolution erected as a tollgate between avowal and the sacred host. A forgotten detail, a concealed item, one fact too much or too little, and my sense of guilt increased tenfold. My adolescence was marked by my endless fears, which isolated me from everyone else. I imagined that teenagers who were more resistant than myself would escape by dodging or lying. But did they also get off scot-free on a psychological level? My refusal to lie whipped up the priest's desire to know, his delight in subjugating young, fragile minds. His bullying simply increased my hatred of all trickery. Being forced to lie and having a tattered conscience are worse than anything. Those painful moments of confession profoundly altered my religious faith.

When I turned seventeen, the Zazou fad was a way of flaunting my difference, my special situation. The confessional no longer received the chronicle of my emotions. I had given up evoking love and pleasure for the selective ears of a manipulative priest. I became sexually active. Soon I learned something important from the other young denizens of Steinbach Square: the existence of a room over a café concert built during the reign of King Louis-Philippe and located on a large downtown plaza near the most elegant stores. A pool table stood at the center of that room, but it was just a front. Sheltered from prying eyes, relations were formed among young men like us and not-so-young ones, with no mention whatsoever of money.

These encounters took place in the afternoon, during the aperitif hour. On the ground floor, smartly dressed patrons, swaying to the strains of a small band, were totally unaware of the pleasures we indulged in over their heads. A far cry from love, these exchanges were purely sexual. The secrecy perfectly suited the city's upper-middle-class homosexuals, who could fulfill their desires without anxiety once the door was locked. They would then go back down to the ground floor, greet acquaintances, and return to their cars, where sometimes a chauffeur would be waiting. These men were highly respected by the local bourgeoisie, which chose to ignore the few nasty rumors about them.

When my watch was stolen on Steinbach Square, I was mortified by the loss of that gift which I valued so greatly. But more than anything, I feared my family's reaction. What could I say if they happened to notice it was gone? I couldn't tell them the truth. As a last resort, I went to the police station to report the theft.

I was received courteously. The policeman had to ask a lot of necessary questions in regard to my statement—but imagine my embarrassment when, realizing the significance of the square and the late hour, he started growing more and more suspicious. I blushed with shame, but I was intent on establishing the facts of the incident. It was the theft that was the crime, and not my sexuality. I signed the complaint, and the officer filed it away.

But just as I was getting up to leave, he told me to sit down again. Then he brutally started using the familiar form with me. How would I feel if my father, a man of great prestige in the city, were to learn where his seventeen-year-old son spent his afternoon? I burst out crying. I didn't want to stain my family's reputation. Today I no longer remember whether those were tears of shame or frustration at being trapped. In any case, I realized how naive I had been to come there, but it was too late. Eventually, after humiliating and frightening me, the police officer grew more reassuring. This time, he said, nothing would come of this compromising affair; I'd simply have to stay away from that disreputable place. Then he let me go. I had entered the police station as a robbery victim, and I left as an ashamed homosexual.

For the time being, the incident had no familial or social consequences. The thief was never found, and all I retained was a sense of malaise. Little did I know that my name was added to the police list of the city's homosexuals, and that three years later my parents would thereby learn the truth about me. And least of all, how could I imagine that this list would deliver me into the hands of the Nazis?

Chapter 2
Schirmeck-Vorbrüch

It was 1939, several months before the outbreak of the war with Germany. On the other side of the Rhine, Hitler had been chancellor for the past six years. In public conversations I heard the word *Jew* more frequently than before; it was pronounced pointedly and emphatically. In the streets of Mulhouse, the members of the Croix de Feu flaunted themselves in regular demonstrations, which led to street brawls. On such days, my parents would close the shutters of the patisserie and shove mattresses up against the windows to shield them from projectiles.

Then France declared war on Germany. My brothers— class of '34, '35, '37, and '39—were mobilized one by one. The phony war—that temporary lull—began. The Maginot Line was our pride; the younger boys in Mulhouse enjoyed biking out there to observe the resentful draftees. We were certain that no military confrontation would occur. Alsace, though threatened by the Reich's greed and vindictiveness, did not realize the danger it was in. The thud of boots and the harangues against the insolence of France, which had to be wiped out, provoked merely our amused and sarcastic comments. The cartoonists had a field day. Our Jewish friends were more nervous; whole Jewish families began leaving Alsace to escape the dangerous proximity of the Reich. A lot of Jews entrusted us with precious objects, which we buried in our cellar for the duration of the war.

As the only son not yet in the army, I grew closer to my sister and my mother. On Sundays, I was given a violet five-franc bill, which sufficed amply for the church offering [given privately to the priest] and for a movie ticket. The Corso was a lovely theater, which had been revamped into a movie house; the balconies allowed certain people to fool around on the floor once the lights were dimmed.

I was put in charge of corresponding regularly with my brothers at the front. My mother would often dictate the contents. As soon as the letters were typed and sealed, I would go to mail them at the railroad station. I have retained that habit of always sending off a letter before nightfall.

Meanwhile I had come a long way in my love life. For several months, I had no longer been content with more or less anonymous and purely sexual encounters. I had met Jo, a young man who was kind and good. We enjoyed spending a lot of time together, isolating ourselves as much as possible from the rest of the world. I told him about my first feelings, the summers in Dieppe, those trips that were really expeditions. And he likewise confided in me. We developed a very powerful bond that neither time nor suffering nor death has erased from my memory.

In June 1940, the phony war turned real. Circumventing the Maginot Line by marching through Belgium, the Germans swarmed over France, meeting little if any resistance. Crossing the Vosges was a mere formality for that army, whose stupefying energy we had all underestimated. They paraded through Mulhouse as victors, with impeccable harnesses, glossy boots, brand-new matériel, and weapons polished to a fault.

Our family wept. Our neighbor was exultant. We thought about all my brothers—we hadn't heard from them since this lightning offensive. After the triumphant German march, long files of French prisoners—a human tide—flooded our streets for many days and nights. They were walking to the Rhine. We handed out June cherries, water, or cakes. The Germans put up with it so long as the prisoners kept moving. The mass was so compact that it swept the prisoners along anyway; they couldn't possibly stop. With blankets over their shoulders, they wearily marched toward POW camps in German territory. My little sister and I watched this parade for hours on end, calling out the first and last names of our brothers. This was one way that some people managed to obtain news. But we learned nothing.

With the defeat of France, the Treaty of Versailles was ripped up, and we found ourselves under the German boot. The new authorities began to expel several hundred thousand undesirables from Alsace. They instantly shut down the cathedral of Strasbourg and threw out the bishop of Metz. The French language and the regional [German] dialects were outlawed. The armistice was signed, but then the three departments of Upper Rhine, Lower Rhine, and Moselle, which had been recovered by France in 1918, were brutally annexed in violation of the Treaty of Versailles. We were fused with greater Germany, integrated into the provinces of Baden and Saar-Palatinate. The administration of our region was taken over by Robert Wagner and Joseph Burkel, two of the Führer's old comrades-in-arms. Orders came directly from Reichsführer Heinrich Himmler, head of the SS, and sometimes even from Hitler himself, for the highest echelons wanted a swift processing of the region.

The new administrative infrastructure was installed practically overnight. Hitler's longtime sympathizers, most of them unknown to us, were given leading positions in the neighborhood. We didn't realize that all these networks had been ready since before the invasion. The collaborators took command without a moment's hesitation.

I had to leave school. From the parochial grade school to the lycée, I had been a good student. My parents would privately debate the future professions of their children before telling us how they felt. It was a matter of identifying our affinities and qualities, then perfecting them after our general studies. For my part, if the war had not upset everything, I would have followed my passion for everything concerning textiles. My parents and I had gotten information about a reputable school in Lille. Along with my secondary studies, I also did internships in several factories. I enjoyed the interplay of the looms and their shuttles. The factory was an exhausting place, demanding a vigilant memory for color—and you also had to swallow a lot of dust—but I wanted to learn more about all aspects of manufacturing, for engineers were greatly in demand. Fashion design also fascinated me; I did lots of sketches for male and female clothing.

The war forced me to rein in my ambitions, however. I had the equivalent of the Abitur, the German high school diploma. I took evening courses, which now had to be taught in German. Nevertheless I managed to earn diplomas in accounting, decorating, and business. Then I found a job as window dresser in a clothing boutique on the rue du Sauvage; owned by a Jew named Schwab, it had been sequestered by the occupation authorities. Sensing graver measures to come, no doubt, the owner had rented several buses, from which he had removed all the seats. He filled the vehicles with the most valuable portion of his stock, evacuating it to his summer home in Belleville-sur-Allier near Vichy. Later on, he made it to America and didn't return home until the Liberation. After my father's death, Schwab purchased our family home on the rue du Sauvage in order to expand his business.

The rue du Sauvage is a highly commercial artery that cuts through the center of Mulhouse. The "savage" is symbolized by the statue of an armored warrior on a corner of a building. At the foot of this building you'll find the Café de l'homme de fer, the Iron Man Café.

One day my father motioned me over to the window. "They're doing something stupid!" he exclaimed. The Nazis were changing the street sign outside our house. The main street in every conquered city was being renamed after their Führer. The rue du Sauvage had become Adolf Hitlerstrasse. Word got around so quickly that all day long people filed past the signs, chortling and guffawing. The "savage" was identified at last. The BBC reported this Nazi gaffe. Aware of their blunder, the authorities renamed the street yet again, translating rue du Sauvage into its literal German equivalent: Wildermann Strasse.

The roundups began. One day the SS came looking for one of the trainees in our pastry shop. We were nervous, for Albert Dreyfus was Jewish. It was rumored that the people arrested that day were being held in the main courtyard of the sub-prefecture and could be seen through the bars. We hurried over. A horrifying spectacle greeted our eyes. We spotted our young apprentice on all fours with other prisoners: they were forced to tear out the grass from between the paving stones and eat it under the kicks and lashes of the SS. On our side of the bars, we felt dumbfounded and powerless. The occupier was intent on showing that he was in full control. We never saw Albert Dreyfus again.

One of my schoolmates had been in the habit of visiting me at home. We had first met in parochial school and had often been rivals in French composition. His father, who was German, ran a major clock store in the center of town. A few days after the invasion, my friend rang our bell: he was wearing a Hitler Youth uniform with a swastika armband. He had come to sing the praises of his organization and wanted me to join. I was too terrified to speak to him, and so he left. For a long time I wondered whether he was one of the people who later denounced me.

Upon taking over the local governments in the occupied areas, the Germans reviewed the contents of the police files. After every territorial defeat, the authorities are obliged to prepare their documents and turn them over to the victor with the transfer of power. But the illegal existence of a homosexual list remains an issue. In 1792, the Napoleonic Code had legalized homosexuality, and the burnings at the stake had ended even earlier. The Vichy government did not pass its anti-homosexual law until 1942.

I was not aware of the terrible fate that the Nazis had been inflicting on German homosexuals since 1933. In Alsace, it was rumored only that homosexuals had been shipped to the border of the free zone, toward Lyon or Bourg-en-Bresse. I remember a friend of mine, a hairdresser in Mulhouse, whose abrupt departure seemed like an expulsion from the territory. The undesirables, who were given very tight deadlines, could take along no more than sixty-five pounds of luggage.

I don't know whether it was an excess of zeal or malevolence that prompted the French authorities to hand over this file with the others. The surveillance of homosexuals is such an inveterate police habit that it probably didn't occur to anyone to terminate it. Furthermore, the invasion had been so sudden that in the ensuing disorder it was probably not very difficult to lay hands on such a list, which, as in Germany, had led to years of easy blackmail, raids, arrests, and the obtaining of information by means of torture and arbitrary internment.

I had no way of knowing what was being hatched in the offices of the Gestapo. I continued going to my evening classes, I spent time with my friend Jo, and I occasionally saw the small group at Steinbach Square. Of course, the enemy, patrolling the streets, had the right to fire at any shadow after curfew, so my nights out were few and far between. In the streets of the city, we sometimes passed other groups as irregular as ours. While a lookout kept watch, these teams ripped down the German posters and replaced them with patriotic calls for resistance. We gladly joined them. Friendship, complicity, and patriotism came together in the night.

From time to time I also returned to the café concert. Occasionally, without a word of explanation, our solid bourgeois homosexuals asked us, the younger ones, to do them a favor—which usually meant carrying a message to someone or other. We likewise mailed mysterious letters for them at the railroad station, where the soldiers on duty didn't notice us because of our youth. We agreed to run those errands unaware of the gravity of what we were doing. In such circumstances, a few teenagers, who were not in any resistance group and who failed to gauge the riskiness of their actions, were arrested, tortured, and shipped off to a concentration camp.

In any case, it must be said that certain homosexuals, those who cruised public squares as well as those older ones who were more discreet, ran varying degrees of risk in acting against the Nazi occupiers. But I was arrested much too early to observe the creation of the resistance networks that soon emerged in Alsace.

Whenever I headed home after work, I would stop off at the patisserie. Even at eighteen, I would gulp down several chocolate eclairs like a child, and my mother would keep track with one eye, for she knew what a terrible sweet tooth I had.

It was May 2, 1941. Behind her cash register, my mother seemed more nervous and preoccupied than usual. She told me that the Gestapo had come by and ordered me to report the following morning. This was not a good sign. She asked me what I had done. I said I didn't know, but I instantly thought of those mysterious letters that I was sometimes asked to mail.

I passed an uneasy night, assailed by all kinds of questions. I knew that the Gestapo could do anything and everything. What was going to happen? What could I have been denounced for, and by whom? I never even remotely thought about another moment in the past— and by the time they refreshed my memory the next day, it was too late.

Early in the morning I presented myself to the Gestapo with my summons. As soon as my name was checked off on a list, I was brutally shoved into a separate room, which rapidly filled up with a dozen young men, some of whom I knew by sight. We waited in silence. Then each of us was brought before a desk in individual rooms.

After violently shutting my file, the SS man facing me instantly called me *Schweinehund* (dirty bastard), filthy faggot. The interrogation was only just starting. Did I know other homosexuals? What were their names and addresses? Had I heard about so-and-so? Wasn't it true that a certain churchman liked young men? Where were our meeting places? He knew a lot more than I did. I remained silent.

The Germans, who obviously knew that I was homosexual, were trying to use me to trap a portion of the city's populace. But what proof did they have of my sexuality? They showed me the statement I had signed at the age of seventeen, when I had told a French police officer about the theft of my watch in a dubious place. There was my signature. I couldn't deny my homosexuality. Others, who could deny theirs, were lucky enough to be expelled from the territory instead of being interned.

The blows came raining down. Behind the desk, each SS man followed the last in an even rhythm. Each time, the grilling started from scratch: last name, first name, date of birth, names and addresses of homosexual acquaintances. One after another the interrogators yelled, threatened, brutalized. They tried to corner us, exhaust us, quell any resistance. After reiterating the same words, the same denials twenty times over, for ten hours in a row, we saw lists emerging from files. We had to sign. Kneeling on a ruler, we had to confirm that all these names made up the roster of homosexuals in Mulhouse. The walls echoed with our screams. Sometimes they took us to a different office, where we were asked to identify other victims who had been rounded up that day. Our eyes met, terrified.

At first we managed to endure the suffering. But ultimately it became impossible. The machinery of violence accelerated. Outraged by our resistance, the SS began pulling out the fingernails of some of the prisoners. In their fury, they broke the rulers we were kneeling on and used them to rape us. Our bowels were punctured. Blood spurted everywhere. My ears still ring with our shrieks of atrocious pain.

When my eyes reopened, I thought I was in the back room of a butcher's shop. I don't know what went through my mind. The torture had overwhelmed even the slightest thought. It was pure violence, the kind that destroys forever. But it was a wretched victory for our torturers. For though I signed the document as others did, to stop the agony, the bloodstains had made it illegible.

Dusk was deepening outside the windows of the Gestapo. At nightfall we were sent to the prison of Mulhouse. I was thrown into a dark, damp, crowded cell. In this tight space, I tried to make room for myself. At the end of that day, the worst day of my life, all I wanted to do was collapse. Around me, a half dozen prisoners moaned or dozed. There were so many that they sat on the ground, leaning against the wall. I had time to see that many of them had likewise been severely tortured: their faces were swollen, their bodies splattered with blood.

After several long minutes, someone offered me a corner in the back of the cell. I went over. It was the worst spot imaginable: water oozed from the wall, and I was absolutely frozen. This welcome for the last arrival, in the most inhospitable corner of the cell, revealed something about the human capacity for solidarity. I thought to myself that while we were victims of the same monstrosities, nothing prevented us from re-creating our normal exclusivity. I couldn't fall asleep until I collapsed in exhaustion.

I spent ten days and ten nights in that tiny space and amid that cruelty. Each prisoner had his own tragedy. Our exchanges were brief, for distrust reigned supreme, and each of us fell back on his own incommunicable suffering. The deprivation of freedom is a monstrosity equaled only by torture.

One of my brothers came to see me in the visitors' room. He and my father, nervous about my disappearance, had gone to the Gestapo the morning after I'd been summoned. There they found out that I was in the city prison. The SS man had added that in any case I was nothing but a *Schweinehund*—the disgusting German word was perfectly understood. And that was how, in the most humiliating manner, my family learned about my homosexuality. A horrible wound, both for them and for me. Moreover, my brother told me that since the Gestapo was a law unto itself, the attorneys they consulted had their hands tied. I was absolutely alone.

At dawn of May 13, 1941, a dozen of us were tossed into a police van that was then padlocked on the outside. The vehicle left the center of Mulhouse, then the suburbs. Where were we going? Peering out the windows, a few prisoners said that we were on the road to Belfort. This could mean that we were being taken to the border and expelled into the free zone—the happiest interpretation. But we had to face the facts: we were heading due north, toward Colmar and Strasbourg or, more precisely, the concentration camp at Schirmeck, in the valley of the Bruche river.

On the road leading to the Donon Pass, some twenty miles west of Strasbourg, a set of barracks had been hastily thrown up by the French during the phony war: they were meant to shelter the people evacuated from the border areas. The Germans had requisitioned all these places, using them to expand the incarceration network in Alsace. On the other side of the Rhine, the various internment structures had been operating for years.

Strasbourg had fallen eleven months earlier, and the Gestapo, installed at police headquarters, had set up countless information networks fed by informers and collaborators. Proportionately, Alsace was the victim of seven times as many imprisonments and deportations as all the rest of France combined. Space was needed for the prisoners. So just a few weeks after the arrival of the Germans, a dozen camps appeared in Alsace: transit, reeducation, internment, and concentration camps. On Monday, July 15, 1940, 150 prisoners from Alsace and elsewhere in France inaugurated the Schirmeck camp.

Schirmeck is not far from the village of La Broque. That's why the camp was also known as Vorbrüch, the German name for La Broque. For the same reason, the concentration camp at Struthof, built one year later by the inmates of Schirmeck—of whom I was one—is some-times called Natzweiller.

As the police van drove up to the entrance of the Schirmeck camp that day in May 1941, we saw barracks surrounded by a double circle of high fences. An obser-vation post towered in each of the four corners. The guards, all German, wore a sinister death's head on their caps and on the facings of their tunics. The van was unlocked and we got out, scared to death. The van sped off.

A torrent of blows awaited us. We were instantly over-come with terror. We had to run, crawl, run, and crawl again. Our civilian clothing was soon reduced to rags. The shouted orders were invariably followed by blows when the SS approached us.

Then, after an icy shower, I had my head shaved like the others. My Zazou hair landed on the floor. The Zazous were obviously despised by the Nazis, who had long since wiped out the German cultural vanguard on the other side of the Rhine, outlawing jazz and any visi-ble signs of any peculiarity. They called them eccentric, destructive of German culture, and disrespectful toward the new order. So as a Zazou, I benefited from a special treatment. The inmate shaving my head left a mark in my skull, for, cutting into the mass of my hair, he had to trace a swastika. That was how I entered the camp, under the eyes of the other prisoners.

Stripped of our torn, filthy clothing, we were handed

camp uniforms: ill-fitting shirts and trousers made of harsh linen. Like several other prisoners from the same van, I noticed a small, enigmatic blue bar on my shirt and my cap. It was part of the indecipherable prison code that was known only to our jailers. According to the documents that I eventually checked, blue meant that I was Catholic or asocial. In this camp, blue also included the homosexuals, while in Germany the homosexual inmates were already marked by the pink triangle. I never wore the pink triangle, nor did I ever see it in Schirmeck, although it appeared later on in the neighboring Struthof camp.

Each inmate had his mark. Those who had a red mark—a triangle, line, or bar—were political prisoners, often Communists. After staying in Schirmeck only briefly, they were soon shipped off to far more terrifying destinations. The same was true of the Jews, who wore a yellow star, and the Gypsies, who wore maroon: their deportation meant extermination.

Schirmeck, which was a *Sicherungslager,* a "security camp," received all kinds of inmates; the only thing they had in common was being the target of Nazi fury. Thus the camp "welcomed" priests, prostitutes, Spanish republicans, deserters from the German army, including some from World War I who had settled on French soil, black-marketeers who had not collaborated sufficiently, and British aviators captured in France.

There were no children behind the barbed wire. What

had they done with them? On the other hand, the rear of the camp—both barracks and washhouse—was reserved for the female inmates, who did the laundry for the SS. Four young volunteers, Alsatian women, were assigned to guard them, and they were as sadistic as the SS men. In the silence of the night, we heard the women prisoners' terrible cries, their weeping and moaning.

I noted that the control of the camp was absolute and that the slightest hint of revolt was crushed on the spot. Escapes from Schirmeck were almost unheard-of. In four years, only one succeeded. Disguised as SS men, four members of a resistance network fled, using one of the black cars in the Gestapo garage. They made it through the gates of the camp and, before the alarm, they managed to erase their trail in the mountains.

If released prisoners were brought back, either because of their recidivism or because they had talked about what they had seen, they received a harsher welcome. Twenty to 180 strokes with a club were inflicted on the penitent, who was tied over a footstool or a barrel. Sometimes the SS covered him with a blanket so that the marks were less visible, but the blows were just as violent.

It was not until two years later that the Alsatian press mentioned the existence of the Schirmeck camp. A newspaper ran a brief item about an Alsatian who had molested a German functionary and then been interned for "reeducation." But rumors had been circulating for a much longer time. In the course of four years, 15,000 Alsatians passed through Schirmeck.

I was spared none of the horrors of Schirmeck. I quickly became a disjointed puppet under the shouts of the SS men, who made me obey all kinds of orders and perform tasks that were exhausting, dangerous, or simply idiotic.

Torn from sleep at six A.M., we wolfed down an indefinable tea and a quarter loaf of stale or moldy *Kommissbrot,* a kind of military sourdough bread. After roll call, most of us headed toward the valley to smash rocks in the surrounding quarries and load the fragments into tiptrucks. The SS brought in German shepherd dogs to dissuade us from fleeing through the dense forest. Other inmates spent eleven hours a day laboring at the Marchal de Wacenbah factory.

Around noon, we were served a clear soup with a slice of sausage. Then work continued until six P.M. Back in the camp, we were systematically searched before reentering our barracks. Two ladlefuls of rutabaga soup ended our day. After a final roll call, our barracks were doubly padlocked, and the night rounds began while the sun had yet to go down behind the mountains.

Exhausted, haggard, I attempted to make eye contact, to say a few words to some of my fellow ghosts, who were as drained as I. But after a few days, I stopped trying. I realized that any communication was impossible, even dangerous: the camp was an anthill, where each person ran to do only his absurd task. We were not allowed to walk normally or to exchange even a few words.

One thing we had to do was pounce on the tiniest scrap of paper lying on the ground and pocket it. The SS men amused themselves by tossing out a piece of paper and watching us fetch it like dogs. At times, certain SS men would throw a scrap toward the prohibited seven-foot margin along the barbed wire, the camp's boundary. The inmates who ran after that scrap were killed for attempting to escape. But if an inmate didn't obey, he was likewise killed for insubordination.

The Sunday morning ritual was personally overseen by the head of the camp, Hauptsturmführer Karl Buck. We had to assemble full-force for roll call. Even the sick had to fall in. They trudged from the infirmary, trembling with fever or on a stretcher. The Sunday dawn inspired Karl Buck.

With the iron cross glinting on his chest, he would launch into an endless tirade about the charms of Nazi Germany, hectoring his reeling audience. We, the dregs of society, had to stop resisting the exciting destiny of the grand Reich. National Socialism had to be our only value. But we were nothing but vermin, and it was a hard chore "reeducating" us. Buck got carried away talking about the misdeeds of religion: the priests, whom his adjutant Robert Wunsch loved working over with a club or a bull's pizzle, were nothing but *Himmelskomiker*, "heavenly comedians." With a nod to the Spanish republican inmates, Buck dwelt on the exemplary struggle against anarchy. Claiming he had fought in the Spanish Civil War, he detailed his heroic acts. He also reminded us that it was quite illusory to try and escape. We listened in silence, surrounded by our jailers. It was impossible to communicate with one another, even in whispers. Not far from the orator, a few corpses often dangled from the gallows, circled by crows: they completed the decor.

In reality, that braggart, that forty-six-year-old brute, had been jobless in 1933 when, like so many others, he joined the NSDAP, the National Socialist German Workers' Party. Two weeks later, he was promoted to SS captain and head of a camp. Before coming to Alsace, he had already run the concentration camps of Heuberg and Welzheim in Germany. He had a wooden leg, which had nothing to do with the Spanish Civil War: it was a souvenir of the humiliating First World War. In moments of exasperation he would use it as a club.

Within a few months Karl Buck doubled the capacity of Schirmeck. Later on, in 1943, he had the inmates build a "party room," an immense building with an outside stairway, its façade adorned with the German eagle and swastika. That edifice could hold up to two thousand people, who would listen to his harangues, which were accompanied by propaganda movies. Underneath the "party room" twenty-six dark cells were built, some of which were used as torture chambers; they were splattered with blood from floor to ceiling. And if any prisoner resisted "reeducation," he was taken, with Himmler's personal endorsement, to have his short life terminated in Stuttgart, where the executions took place. This formality was superfluous for Russians and Poles, who could be killed at any time. Their files would simply contain the usual formula: "Killed while attempting to escape."

After the roll call and the speech, we returned to our forced labor; we always had to run. I don't recall having walked even once in that inhuman space, where some six hundred people were herded together. If we didn't go to the quarry, we stayed in the camp. We had to level the roads between the barracks by dragging a roller whose straps cut into our bellies. We also had to scrub all the barracks with floods of water or tend the flower beds under the commandant's windows. Everything in the camp had to be irreproachable and the reports to Berlin full of praise. Karl Buck sometimes invited local authorities, collaborators, to view his handiwork, and their reports had to be enthusiastic.

But when there were no visitors, Karl Buck never went on foot inside the camp. He got behind the wheel of his black Citroën and tooled along the roads. Prisoners had to throw themselves on the shoulder of the road while not forgetting to salute the Hauptsturmführer. He would sometimes injure a less attentive or less agile man, for the black thunderbolt would hurtle around a barrack and never stop.

Overhead loudspeakers transmitted classics—Bach, Beethoven, Wagner—and military marches. That background music would be interrupted by a voice ordering Prisoner So-and-so to report to the authorities, the washhouse, or the infirmary. Sometimes they summoned me. They had to wrap up my file, which had been opened at the Mulhouse Gestapo. I was asked the same questions. Didn't I have anything to add? According to them, my meager knowledge of the manners and mores of homosexuals in my town was unsatisfactory. My youth must have given me access to secrets that were of interest to them. Why this stupid resistance? They gladly reminded me that they had all the time in the world to get more out of me.

Because of the altitude, the nights were cool during that spring of 1941. At the center of each barrack was a black stove which, on good days, was used to cook food that someone had chanced upon; these surprises eased our starvation. The barrack was made up of networks of various affinities, some political, which slightly reduced the isolation and hardship of everyday life. I was not part of any of these solidarity groups. With my blue ribbon, which was quickly interpreted by my fellow unfortunates, I realized I could expect nothing from them. Sexual crime is an added burden for a prisoner's identity. (I could verify this later on, during the period when I worked as a prison inspector in Rouen.) In the universe of inmates, I was a completely negligible element that could be sacrificed at any moment, indifferently, depending on the random demands of our jailers.

At the end of each day, after our physical and mental ordeals, we collapsed on our straw pallets, famished and exhausted. Each barrack, initially designed for 45 inmates, was crowded with up to 140. The wooden bunks had two, then three levels. The pallets, lying right on the slats, were merely sacks of straw, producing a lot of dust that was inhaled by the sleeper. The bunks that were highest, but also closest to the stove, were obviously the most desired. Often our jailers, looking for possible hiding places, would dump everything on the ground or even make us change barracks with no explanation. And then the battle for beds would start all over again. It was hard-fought, because our environment made our few hours of sleep very precious.

For a while I had a young man underneath who wheezed very heavily at night and was shaken by frequent attacks of asthma. The infirmary had given him eucalyptus cigarettes to calm his respiration, but they had been stolen by other prisoners. He didn't dare complain, and so his nightly fits got worse and worse, preventing many inmates from sleeping. As luck would have it, at that very moment some prisoners had stolen a few precious crusts of bread from the evening ration; the young asthmatic was publicly accused of that theft by the inmates responsible for maintaining order in the barrack.

The unfortunate man denied the unjust charge. He was well aware of the reprisals he was inexorably threatened with. But if he'd complained to the SS, the punishment would have been worse. Instead he was put in a sack, which each of us then had to kick in turn, with varying degrees of cruelty. Each kick, more or less aimed at a specific part of the body—the head or the genitals by the most ferocious—served as a personal outlet to pay back the violence that we all had to endure. With a swollen face and a bloody body, the victim dragged himself to the infirmary. He soon left our barrack and disappeared. A short time later, we heard that he had died.

As one of the youngest inmates, I was afraid that attention would focus on me. So between periods of labor, I made sure not to talk to anyone, locking myself up in a desperate solitude untouched by any sexual desire. In that place, there was no room for even the thought of desire. A ghost has no fantasies, no sexuality. Each of us thus had to remain alone amid the crowd. During rare moments when we could stare at one another in silence, I noted a few acquaintances (aside from the men who'd been in the police van on May 13, 1941). But it was hard to recognize them, for our clothes, our shaved heads, and our starved bodies had erased each man's age and identity. He had become a staggering shadow of himself.

Reduced to mute observation, I naturally spotted affinities, complicities; but they were exceedingly rare. For example, I remember two Czechs—lovers from before, no doubt—who occasionally managed to exchange a few words by facing a window of our barrack. With their backs toward the others, they could see someone coming in the reflection of the glass. But the haphazard jumble of people and the denunciations left little room for even the slightest gesture of humanity. There was some trafficking in cigarettes and stubs—but the punishment for anyone caught with tobacco was twenty-five lashes of the whip and two weeks in solitary.

We tried to resist the extreme cruelty and degradation inflicted on us. What passed for hygiene was restricted to a trickle of icy water outside our barrack. Inside, vermin had attacked the bedding. To treat the injuries caused by their ordeals, the prisoners used makeshift bandages, which then infected their wounds. But no one cared. The only value was violence. Beating was the principle activity of the SS. Once, inflicting reprisals on the entire camp, they had to stop at the fourth barrack—they were exhausted and out of breath!

I soon came down with dysentery and acute rheumatism in my hands. The belt of the roller we used to level the roads in the camp gave me violent pains in the belly. As for my legs, they were so overworked that they were ruined for good. Even today, I am sometimes bedridden with bleeding legs for days on end.

From time to time the infirmary summoned me for treatment. The doctor was very kind. He came from the surrounding area and had, no doubt, been forced into this position. While taking my pulse, he would cautiously sneak a tiny piece of chocolate into my sleeve. After the war, I tried to find him, but the inhabitants of his village could not or would not tell me anything. Perhaps he became a collaborator. Or perhaps his activity at the camp was viewed as criminal. If he had any problems after the Liberation, I'm sorry that I couldn't testify to his kindness and the risks he took to remain human amid those atrocities. For the SS were always watching him.

I was terrified whenever my name came booming out of the loudspeakers, for sometimes the authorities wanted to inflict monstrous experiments on me. Mostly these consisted of very painful injections in my nipples. There were half a dozen of us, bare-chested and lined up against the wall. I have very clear memories of white walls, white shirts, and the laughter of the orderlies. The orderlies enjoyed hurling their syringes at us like darts at a fair. During one injection session, my unfortunate neighbor blacked out and collapsed: the needle had struck his heart. We never saw him again.

One of the worst things that haunted each day was hunger. It was carefully maintained by our jailers and was the source of countless fights. Starvation roamed the camp, turning us into animals, forcing us to run considerable risks. Sometimes, when I was assigned to clean the rabbit hutches, I surreptitiously wolfed down a few carrots. Once, during yet another third degree, the SS officer approached us with a spoonful of jam. All we had to do was tell him what he wanted to hear and then, he said, we could taste that delicious treat. He was so furious at failing to break our resistance that he hurled the spoon across the room.

Hunger drove some of us insane. I remember an inmate who was often in the "toilet"—a few planks over a smelly hole into which the feeblest men would sometimes slip. This inmate would linger here, where lots of flies gathered. Whenever he succeeded in catching one, he would choke back little cries of contentment.

Sunday brought a further torture, which our captors greatly relished in good weather. While we labored, the SS set up tables groaning with food outside their house. The aromas of the banquet wafted over to us, making our heads spin. The SS feasted noisily for all of us to see. They particularly appreciated the Alsatian wine. The sun and the summer heat lent a golden glow to that monstrous scene. The scraps of the banquet would have been enough for us; we would have gladly devoured them on all fours. The SS men got drunk and roared with laughter. Their imaginations were stoked, fired up, and they vied with one another. The outdoor feast would sometimes end with some improvised sadistic games at our expense.

Soon the Schirmeck camp was completely full, like all the other detention centers in Alsace. Their capacity had to be expanded. At Himmler's express orders, the authorities had to speed up the construction of the Struthof concentration camp on the mountain two thousand feet above us. We had to clear the area, remove the pebbles and rocks, and carry in tree trunks. Others built the barracks. Our labor unit climbed uphill, in trucks or on foot in the forest, herded together by the German shepherd dogs. They didn't always send out the same inmates, for they didn't want us to catch on too quickly to the purpose of this building site. This was a waste of effort on the part of our captors—we soon recognized one of the things that they were forcing us to build: a crematorium. As our eyes took it in, horrified whispers accompanied our monstrous discovery.

Days, weeks, months wore by. I spent six months, from May to November 1941, in that place, where horror and savagery were the law. But I've put off describing the worst ordeal I suffered. It happened during my earliest weeks in the camp and contributed more than anything else to making me a silent, obedient shadow among the others.

One day the loudspeakers ordered us to report immediately to the roll-call site. Shouts and yells urged us to get there without delay. Surrounded by SS men, we had to form a square and stand at attention, as we did for morning roll call. The commandant appeared with his entire general staff. I assumed he was going to bludgeon us once again with his blind faith in the Reich, together with a list of orders, insults, and threats—emulating the infamous outpourings of his master, Adolf Hitler. But the actual ordeal was far worse: an execution. Two SS men brought a young man to the center of our square. Horrified, I recognized Jo, my loving friend, who was only eighteen years old. I hadn't previously spotted him in the camp. Had he arrived before or after me? We hadn't seen each other during the days before I was summoned by the Gestapo.

Now I froze in terror. I had prayed that he would escape their lists, their roundups, their humiliations. And here he was, before my powerless eyes, which filled with tears. Unlike me, he had not carried dangerous letters, torn down posters, or signed any statements. And yet he had been caught and he was about to die. What had happened? What had the monsters accused him of? Because of my anguish I have completely forgotten the wording of the death sentence.

Then the loudspeakers broadcast some noisy classical music while the SS stripped him naked and shoved a tin pail over his head. Next they sicced their ferocious German shepherds on him: the guard dogs first bit into his groin and thighs, then devoured him right in front of us. His shrieks of pain were distorted and amplified by the pail in which his head was trapped. My rigid body reeled, my eyes gaped at so much horror, tears poured down my cheeks, I fervently prayed that he would black out quickly.

Since then I sometimes wake up howling in the middle of the night. For fifty years now that scene has kept ceaselessly passing and repassing through my mind. I will never forget that barbaric murder of my love — before my very eyes, before *our* eyes, for there were hundreds of witnesses. Why are they still silent today? Have they all died? It's true that we were among the youngest in the camp and that a lot of time has gone by. But I suspect that some people prefer to remain silent forever, afraid to stir up hideous memories, like that one among so many others.

As for myself, after decades of silence I have made up my mind to speak, to accuse, to bear witness.

Chapter 3
Destination Smolensk

November 1941. The hellish rhythm of the camp—repetitious days punctuated by incessant bullying—had long since settled into my body, into my mind. Nothing happened, aside from the daily cycle of atrocities blithely programed by the SS. Autumn had followed summer. The forest around us glowed. Beyond the barbed wire and the watchtowers, nature, we saw, was flaunting her lavish beauty. Often, while gazing at the Vosges, which were beginning to turn white with snow, I wished that something would happen—anything, no matter how awful, so long as it put an end to this routine of debasement, this machinery of abuse.

Sometimes as the morning haze dissolved I would look, along with the other inmates, at a statue of the Virgin that stood on one of the crenelated towers of the castle in the valley, by the side of a mountain. The eyes of several prisoners converged in that direction. We said nothing, but I know what filled my mind and, no doubt, those of my companions: the only thought that was still a bit coherent—the thought of going home, finding our loved ones, sleeping in our own beds, our own rooms. Going home.

One day in November 1941, I heard my name from the loudspeakers. They were summoning "Seel, Peter" to the commandant. Several days earlier, after raking the gravel at the entrance, I had again been assigned to clean the hutches, and there I had managed to filch a few carrots meant for the rabbits. Had someone spotted me and turned me in? I could be hanged. Or was I to be interrogated yet again? Or receive more injections? Or be transferred to another camp? Having long since abandoned the very notion of resisting their decisions, I had to submit with apprehension but also with an overwhelming fatalism. In such a hell, hope had become an aberrant idea.

Karl Buck sat behind his desk. He didn't seem particularly enraged—at most he seemed distrustful. Contrary to habit, he didn't yell. His tone was grave, his speech ceremonious. Going by his henchmen's reports on my attitude in the camp, he had concluded that I could leave because of my good conduct. I could now become a fullfledged German citizen. I would even be permitted to say "Heil Hitler" when leaving his office—a privilege reserved for well-behaved men in the Reich. Standing at attention before him, I couldn't believe my ears—I wondered if it was a trap?

One last formality. On his desk, in front of me, a green document stamped with the German eagle awaited my signature. Buck's tone now turned more menacing: "Be sure you understand: if you are tempted to drop even the slightest hint about what you have experienced or seen in this camp, if you disappoint the authorities of the Reich, you will obviously find yourself behind barbed wire again."

Calmly but very firmly, he was demanding my complete silence. I was flabbergasted, stunned. But I obeyed and I signed without reading. Buck took back the document and placed it in his safe.

What had I signed? That question has haunted me for a long time. And it terrorized me all the while I was a German citizen, then a German soldier. Perhaps I remembered the complaint I had filed two years earlier at the Mulhouse police station. There too I had signed without reflecting, and that had been the start of my tragedy. But this time, in the camp, I had no other choice than to sign. It was an order. Perhaps it was also a sinister farce; perhaps I'd be killed the instant I stepped through the gates of the camp.

After I signed the document, Karl Buck remained the same. Suddenly, I was filled with the wild hope that his proposition was "honest." I saluted as agreed and, following his orders, I headed toward the depot. There they gave me back my civilian clothes in exchange for my camp uniform—my mended and tattered cap, shirt, and trousers, and their terrible bar of color. I received money to buy a train ticket for Mulhouse. Then, without turning my head to cast a final glance at my companions in misfortune, I walked through the barred gate.

I was not killed. Among the streets of Schirmeck, the road to the railroad station seemed to stretch out forever. I felt that my shaved head and my gauntness were drawing stares, which weighed me down. I was eighteen, but I had no age. My love had died; the Nazis had left me in tatters. One hour earlier, not far from the gallows, I had been performing mindless, robotic actions amid the shrieks, the dogs, the machine guns, and the watchtowers.

Why had the Nazis released me? What were they going to demand of me next? It was all so incredible. And what if they decided to use me as cannon fodder? I was supposed to report to the Mulhouse Gestapo every morning. Toward what end? What was in that document that I had signed? My pledge of silence? Or my German citizenship?

When I got off the train in Mulhouse, I stupidly looked around, as if my family would be there to pick me up after being courteously informed by my Nazi jailers. No such luck, of course. Walking through the streets of my hometown was equally painful. The rumors about roundups of homosexuals must have spread citywide.

And after I had been taken from them, my family had learned that I was a "*Schweinehund.*" How would my parents react, as Catholics concerned about their reputation? Would they welcome me or not? And in what way? And what could I tell them, how could I explain, since I had a gag order? I told myself that the entire family would go along with my father's attitude.

And that was what happened. When I arrived at our front door, I rang like a stranger. I saw someone leaning out the window to see who it was. Did they recognize me? There were no shouts. I can't remember who came down to open the door. I managed to climb the stairs and cross the threshold of the dining room.

My family was at the table. My father stood up. As I advanced, he took his gold watch from his vest pocket and handed it to me, saying, "Here, son, this is my welcome-home present. Sit down with us. We won't say anything more about it. And then you'll have a rest."

The housekeeper pulled a chair over and set a place. I could sit down among my loved ones. The meal proceeded in silence. At the other end of the table, I saw my mother trying to choke back her tears. No one broke the hush.

It was November 6, 1941. Two secrets had been unsealed simultaneously: the Nazi horror and the shame of my homosexuality. From time to time, a glance swept over me, a silent inquiry about my starved appearance. What had become of me during those six months? So I was a homosexual? What had the Nazis put me through? Why had they set me free? No one asked those obvious questions. But if anyone had asked, I wouldn't have answered: I was forced to keep my double secret. And it has taken me forty years to reply to those silent glances.

I went to my room, my books, my things—all part of a distant identity, from before my annihilation. Between the silken sheets on my bed, in an ideal warmth, I felt horribly oppressed. I could only sleep on the carpet. That night, driven by a terrifying hunger, I attacked the pantry. My family decided to padlock all the food cupboards. My nocturnal shrieks as I awoke from my nightmares roused the entire household. Doctors came to treat my dysentery.

The morning after my return, I began reporting to the Gestapo. That was my great terror. What if I were rearrested? I left at the crack of dawn to avoid the stares of passersby. Then I returned straight home and kept to my room for the rest of the day. I was still frightened by everything, for that familiar calm was deceptive: I could be snatched away at any moment. I was unable to realize that I was still alive. And was I really?

Four months dragged by like that. Since I was never detained by the Gestapo, I started believing that they would forget me. Yet I had learned that the Nazis had invaded the Soviet Union five months earlier. Germany was now battling on all fronts. For its war machine and its industry, it had to draw on all reserves, no matter where. As a full-fledged citizen of the Reich, I could expect to be drafted sooner or later.

I still slept on my bedroom floor. My health improved somewhat. But I didn't want to see anybody. What could I tell them? Schirmeck existed only in rumors. Nothing about the tortures and killings. Nothing about the gallows, the summary executions, Karl Buck's harangues, the hunger, the misery, nothing about the people cooped up there in the winter cold, nothing about the humiliation, the sadism of the SS. As for the crematorium at the Struthof camp, it was already operating at full throttle, burning the first resistance networks into ashes that settled upon the snowy evergreens of the Vosges.

Outside the camp, the news was no less alarming. After my imprisonment in Schirmeck, Vichy outlawed Free-Masonry, authorized the arrest and administrative internment of reputedly "dangerous" people, and proclaimed the anti-Jewish laws. Admiral Jean-Louis-Xavier-François Darlan, who was Pétain's "dauphin," demanded a list of all people averse to collaborating while—*propagande oblige*—the ashes of Napoleon II were placed in the Pantheon. But Great Britain was still holding out, and a domestic resistance was organizing on French soil. The United States, awakened by Pearl Harbor, finally joined the war. The European conflict was now global. All at once, the Germans needed more manpower. There was no way they would leave Alsace alone.

The first day of spring, March 21, 1942, I received a German draft notice. A soldier detailed to the conscription effort brought it to my parents' house. I was assigned to the RAD, the Reichsarbeitsdienst (Reich Labor Force). That dismal document, like my summons to the Gestapo ten months earlier, augured nothing good. The family cocoon is very fragile when confronted with the violence of nations.

Like other men, I tried to avoid that additional ordeal. I had heard that you could get out of it if you made yourself very sick by eating sardines laced with aspirin. The results would be white foam on the lips and awful breath, and all you had to do was add some theatrical spasms. It worked for a few men. But I flopped. They wouldn't believe me.

So it was off to war at eighteen and a half, and in a German uniform. I can't remember my departure from Mulhouse; as for the subsequent three years, when I crisscrossed Europe in every direction, lots of dates, places, and details now escape me completely. No matter how hard I try to recall and pinpoint the events, they elude me. Forgotten? Repressed? It's as if I concentrated all my willpower on surviving and not on remembering. All that's left are random snatches of memory, unsettling in their disorder.

Together with Czechs and Austrians, I was billeted in a RAD barracks in Vienna. I recall that there were a lot of us from Alsace, Lorraine, and Luxembourg. The officers were all Prussian, many from Pomerania.

One of them took me on as an orderly. I polished his boots, fixed his meals, and took care of his affairs and his horse. I wonder whether this assignment wasn't deliberate on the part of the Nazis: my file had obviously followed me, and my officer knew about it. He knew where I came from and why. Thus he could supervise me constantly, observe my attitude, and verify my silence. I very quickly resumed the gestures of obedience I had learned in Schirmeck.

There followed six months of paramilitary training. We were being prepared for war. But the army was prudent enough not to teach us how to use real weapons, giving us instead the *Spaten* — a long spade that we handled for hours on end, pretending it was a gun. It was so heavy that it left huge calluses on our palms. We were also taught how to goose-step. We wore khaki uniforms with boots and a cap or kepi. But the most humiliating thing of all was being forced to wear the swastika armband.

I was fascinated by the Austrian capital: the cathedral, the Prater, the pastry shops. Despite the war, this city continued flaunting its legendary splendors, its elegant nights. During gala events the Opera was surrounded by as many gawkers as happy guests. On my evenings off, I loved watching this sophisticated hubbub, the stylish clothing and the refined elegance. Those marks of civilization contrasted with the brutishness of our military life.

I recall a burst of fleeting happiness in that distinguished setting during that gloomy spring. At the bottom of the stairs, a woman left the group she was with and offered me an invitation to the performance. Why, and why me? I don't know. I must have spoken a few words of embarrassed gratitude, wondering whether or not I should kiss the hand of that apparition in evening gown and fur. She laughed, perhaps noticing my accent, and replied before vanishing: "Why, you're French!" Her smile was strange and warm.

A few seconds later I entered the opera house that had welcomed the greatest composers in Europe and I watched the opera; but today I can't even remember its name. However—and the memory of it still arouses my emotions today—the chorus sang the Lord's Prayer.

Another happy episode comes to mind; it is equally odd, for once again I have forgotten the circumstances. I had become friendly with a Czech who was likewise in our barracks for RAD training. I hadn't told him very much about myself, for I wasn't trying to make any solid contacts. Was he touched by my sadness or moved by my silence? In any case, he suggested that I go on furlough in his place and visit his wife.

I have nurtured an idyllic memory of those days in the Bavarian Alps—three days of sleep, strolls, and generous meals. I was grateful to his wife for taking me in, but I nevertheless felt I was in a bizarre situation. She had been expecting her husband, and I had arrived in his stead. Still we had a nice rapport. I returned to the barracks with cakes for everyone and made sure of noting that generous comrade's address. I subsequently wrote him several times, but war scatters mail, and I lost track of him. What ever became of him and his wife? I would have liked to stay in touch so that, after the madness, we could have chatted quietly about all those things and shared our memories.

We were yanked out of Vienna and shipped to the Rhineland, winding up in Gütersloh, near the Dutch border. It was a barracks attached to an immense military airfield that sent planes toward Great Britain. During that summer of 1942, when I turned nineteen, I once again became an officer's orderly. But this did not exempt me from the troops' labors.

Every morning, we biked out to one of the building sites on that military airfield. Our bikes had no brakes; to stop you were supposed to pedal in reverse. I found this completely incomprehensible because my relationship to my body had long since been distorted, indeed destroyed. Riding in single file, our wheels almost grazing, our convoy would start out at dawn. The company, naturally, had assigned its youngest member to lug the mess plates for lunch. Weighted down with the luncheon hardware, I brought up the rear.

One day, loaded with my cargo, I found myself skidding downhill, unable to perform the right action for braking. I crashed on the shoulder, knocking down the bike ahead of me, which, in a domino effect, brought down almost the entire company. A report was filed. I was sentenced to practice biking every evening after work. I was ordered to ride around the airfield amid the roar of the planes landing and taking off, while my trainer kept shouting, "*Schneller, schneller!*" — faster, faster!

At the end of my six months of "military preparation" I returned to Mulhouse on September 26, 1942. But my joy was short-lived. My parents told me that the Germans had issued a decree for the systematic conscription of Alsatians and Lorrainers into the Wehrmacht. The Nazi boots had thus trampled on the Hague Convention. So I was not surprised when my new orders arrived: I was to report at the ticket window of the Mulhouse railroad station on the fifteenth of the month.

I had only nineteen days of respite, nineteen days during which, once again, I shut myself up in my room. Events were coming thick and fast. The Germans had launched the mass arrests of Jews in the large cities of occupied France. As for the "free" zone, it would survive for only another few weeks.

Meanwhile, after six months of internment and six months in the RAD, my nightmare was to continue. This time I would not escape combat. The horrors I had already seen and suffered in the concentration camp would be inflicted on me throughout Europe. For three years, I became a ghost in the service of death.

Someday historians will have to recount the monstrous tale of the unwilling Alsatians and Lorrainers who were forced to kill resisters, anti-Fascists, and their families—in short, murder the enemies of the Reich. The humiliating statute of August 25, 1942, tolled the death knell for the patriotic pride of Alsatian youth, which was forced to sacrifice itself to the Nazi flag. Even today France still does not really care to know about and acknowledge the horror of our forced mission.

So on October 15, 1942, my family accompanied me to the station. My mother was weeping: I was only twenty and I was once again leaving for hell. I joined my fellow unfortunates with a raging heart. At the ticket window, the MPs separated us from our loved ones. In the jostling, our hugs were awkward and our final words were drowned out by the din. The Wehrmacht had exclusive access to the platforms where our trains were waiting. The ambiance was electric; the SS men overseeing the departure of the draftees kept reexamining our papers and yelling twice as loud as usual. Nor did the men wearing the uniform of the Feldgendarmerie, the military police, lag behind them. They quickly herded us toward our trains, no doubt to avoid any collective disobedience and to prevent any escapes. The doors of the railroad cars were shut, and the train, groaning, got under way.

Driven from the station for the last farewells, the families had regrouped on the two bridges over the tracks. We all pressed against the windows of the train, sticking our heads out, seeking beloved silhouettes at the railings.

For one last time, we all waved a hand or a handkerchief, even in the void. What counted most was the farewell gesture itself, whether or not it was spotted.

Which of us now began singing the *Marseillaise?* I don't know. In any case he was joined by a vocal mass: at first it rumbled softly from car to car, then it blared out as the train chugged under the bridges where our families were thronged. The SS, pointing their weapons at us, yelled for the windows to be closed. But we ignored them. We sang at the top of our lungs, delighting and terrifying our families with our patriotic gesture, which even Radio London talked about. Suddenly, in Colmar, machine guns awaited us on the station platform. Then came Strasbourg, Kehl, and the crossing of the Rhine: the Reich, the plunge into the war.

Our final destination was Yugoslavia via Austria. The Germans had invaded Yugoslavia eighteen months earlier, and its widespread underground was fighting back harder than ever. Serbia, allied with Tito, was harassing the German army and its friends, the Croats. I have forgotten the details, the place names, the overall context. But I very clearly remember that we regularly left Zagreb on punitive expeditions, armed with grenades, to pursue those diehard resisters into the surrounding mountains. Their resistance exasperated the Germans, who increased their operations. For the road to Greece should have been "normalized" long ago. Tito's *maquis* was more vigorous than had been foreseen, and the atrocities committed by the Nazis merely reinforced the resistance, which gained the support of wider and wider segments of the population.

When I talk about the following, I still feel a deep shame. The anti-Nazi resisters, retreating into their mountains, moved rapidly, using the terrain more flexibly than the German army they were harassing. The Nazi response was monstrous. As we pushed through isolated villages containing only women and children, we had to burn down the thatched-roof houses. The women's shrieks reached us from those dreadful furnaces. One day, disgusted by these terrible vendettas that we were forced to carry out, we told our superiors that we had all lost our cigarette lighters. That very evening, our bread rations were withheld; instead we got matches.

Another day, alas, I found myself, as I might have expected, facing a partisan at a turn in a precipitous road. We were too close to shoot. With the butt of his rifle, he smashed my jaw. But I didn't lose consciousness; I managed to strike back. It was either him or me. The Nazis had taught us to kill, then forced us to kill. They had turned us into murderers.

Seriously wounded, I succeeded in rejoining my company. I was shipped to the rear and admitted to a country hospital of the Red Cross. Later on, I lost all my teeth. But it was doubtless owing to my wounds that I wasn't immediately returned to the front lines like the others. As an auxiliary soldier, with no precise specialty, no qualification useful to the Reich, I was transferred to Berlin. I became a pencil-pusher in the barracks, still wearing the uniform of the Wehrmacht. I was obsessed with keeping the lowest possible profile, so I engaged only in small talk with my comrades. Hunched over my papers, I silently counted the passing weeks, dreaming only about going home.

In early 1943, Berlin, the nerve center of a Europe put to fire and sword, displayed an extraordinary vitality despite the raging war. Once again, as in Vienna, I could stroll about, sometimes go to a restaurant, and observe the distant lights of great festivities. I was not long in noting the quasi-total disappearance of homosexuals. I was unaware that ten years earlier all the night spots had been emptied of their habitués, all the organizations outlawed, and their thousands of members arrested by a special unit of the Gestapo. Those who had a record or were on a police list had been the first to be rounded up. The largest center of homosexual archives and associations, a brainchild of Magnus Hirschfeld, had been sacked long ago by the SA. Denunciations did the rest.

Spring 1943 was approaching. From where we were, it was very difficult to find out how far the Reich had gone. Both the army and the populace seemed to be supporting their leader more ardently than ever. The propaganda was going full-blast. On every street corner, every shop window, a swastika, a portrait of the Führer, or a slogan was a reminder, as if one was needed, of the regime that

Germany was living under. The Berliners seemed perfectly adjusted to it.

From that gray existence I was leading then, a strange, unsettling memory flares up. I pinpointed it only recently in a bookstore, when I was leafing through a book on Nazi Germany, *For the Sake of the Race.* The subject, accompanied by photos, was the *Lebensborn.* Suddenly I stopped at one photo that jogged my memory: it was the *Lebensborn* in Bad Polzin, Pomerania.

There were a dozen such institutions in the Reich. The name, made up out of whole cloth, was a typical Nazi neologism combining *Leben* (life) and *Born* (wellspring). The wellspring of life, the fountain of youth, was actually a factory for blond babies created by mating carefully selected partners "of pure Aryan stock." The babies endured a crude baptismal ceremony at an altar sporting a swastika, with SS men standing at attention by the cradle. The birth certificates all listed the same father: Adolf Hitler. One morning in that spring of 1943, the authorities ordered me to go and stay in Pomerania, some three hundred miles northeast of Berlin. I was not told why. In uniform and with my *Befehl,* the obligatory document for all traveling, I reported to the sentries at a gate surmounted by a fluttering swastika flag. Beyond the wall, I saw an immense park filled with greenery and flowers, birds and fountains. It was dotted with isolated cottages — love nests toward which scantily dressed couples were walking with their arms around each other.

Upon entering the central building, I presented my ID card once again. My welcome was extremely courteous. They took me to my room, handing me the program of festivities, mealtimes, and the facilities of the place. The room was richly furnished and comfortable. Next to the bed I found something that was a technological master-piece for the era: a miniature radio you could place in your ear and that, needless to say, broadcast the propa-ganda of the national network. (Later on I came across that modern gadget in certain military hospitals of the Reich.) Through the window I saw carefree couples strolling, utterly absorbed in their idylls. The men, all blond and well-built, were bare-chested.

At noon, I went to the dining room. An imposing size, with its chandeliers and carpets, its fine tablecloths and napkins, it was worthy of a palace. The trained staff mem-bers were older, and some of them wore white gloves. The service was apparently performed by prisoners. The tables were scattered about. All you had to do was choose a seat, and everyone at the table stood up at your arrival to welcome you with a thunderous "Heil Hitler!" Then the meal was served in all due form. Greatly intrigued, I wondered about these young, handsome men who had their protective arms around one or more women. In a recessed area, a chamber ensemble alternately played classical and military music. Where was I?

It didn't dawn on me until I heard the welcoming

speech, which was followed by a slide show. I was witnessing one of the Reich's long-term programs: its goal was to put an end to marriage and family by creating a direct link between procreation and Nazism. Hitler's ideology was to become eternal, and so, in these paradisal places, beautiful children were to be conceived according to the racial standards of the Third Reich. The parents were selected among beautiful young people, who were proud to be carrying out their mission of anonymous procreation. Off to the side, in the park, a birth clinic and a nursery received the fruits of these programmed encounters. With SS men guarding the entrances, these buildings were under the aegis of nurses and wetnurses in coifs and long black dresses. I was terrified by this quasi-animal breeding. Giving the Führer a son was a sacred, exciting mission: the propaganda had done its job.

I couldn't figure out what I was doing here: I was anything but a blond Aryan and I was certainly listed as a homosexual. And if I had felt any sexual desire, it obviously wouldn't have been for these women. Why did they want me to know about this project, which was so dear to Himmler, its fervent architect? Was I meant to go back to my barracks and rave about the delights of National Socialism to my incredulous or jealous comrades? Or was I to complete my "reeducation"? Was I supposed to be convinced of the value of heterosexuality? Was I to blanch before the beauty of these plump Gretchens? As for the men, who were proud to be chosen and to be here, I dreaded their empty blue eyes. They didn't interest me in the least.

It wasn't until later that I found out the truth about these so-called paradisal Lebensborn centers. They were filled with thousands of blond Norwegian women who had been rounded up to serve as fertile wombs for the Reich. I also learned that Himmler had sent out monstrous kidnappers, who tracked down young blond heads throughout northern Europe. They would round up children in the middle of the street, snatching them from their parents and tossing them into trucks. Did my superiors plan to seduce me with their filthy schemes, to lead me away from my homosexuality and turn me into a kidnapper of boys? Did they want to make me one of the perverse monsters combing Scandinavia? Today that hypothesis strikes me as unreal. But then what value did my superiors place on sending me here? What were they trying to tell me? I still haven't a clue. All I know is that after the war the German and the Alsatian press ran two-page spreads listing these lost children of the Reich, who were searching for their parents; the language was bureaucratic, but nonetheless touching.

I returned to Berlin still very puzzled by those allegedly idyllic days. Above all, I had focused on sleeping and eating, and when I was back in the barracks, I was very stingy with information. In any case, no interview, no training course came of that strange trip.

Nevertheless, my return to the imperious summons of roll call was a rude shock. The shouting was incessant, even in issuing the daily list of orders and duties.

On an early-summer morning in 1943, they asked for volunteers who could write and do arithmetic. This time — I don't know why — I raised my hand, even though my father had drilled into me: "Don't ever volunteer. They'll assign you horrible chores. You'll rue the day!" Once, on the Croatian front, they had asked for six men to go in search of bread. A lot of men volunteered, hoping to bag a few crusts. They had returned reeling and blanching, having been deployed as an execution squad.

Later during that summer day in 1943, the loudspeakers informed me that "Seel, Peter" was being summoned by the noncommissioned officers. As I recall, I already regretted my audacity, and, as usual, my fear returned, making my knees tremble.

No real deceit was involved. I was detailed for a crash course at the Reichsbank in Berlin. Then I was attached to a brigade whose job was to ride the furlough trains between Belgrade and Salonika and exchange German marks for drachmas and vice versa. This transfer had an official rate, which served as our reference. I counted the money. At each terminal, I went to the Reichsbank office. The receipts were placed in a padlocked wooden box, and I was escorted by two soldiers. Then, set free for a couple of hours without surveillance, I mailed postcards in French to my parents even though we were not allowed to use that language. A few cards made it past the censors. I found several of them recently.

As in the previous year, I spent the winter in the Yugoslav mountains. I took forty-two round trips over the three hundred miles between Belgrade and Salonika. Often British planes would fly low and strafe us, and sometimes Tito's partisans would blow up the tracks. Once, an attack blocked our train in a tunnel. I remember asphyxiating smoke and dreadful shrieks under a dark, oppressive vault.

Because of my duties, I rode in the officers' car, where travel conditions were less harsh than in the troop cars. A generous tip induced the cook to favor us. Corruption was rampant. The officer I worked for would be wearing a new gold ring every time he returned from Salonika. One day I got up enough nerve to ask him about it. He snapped, "None of your business, it's a secret." Indeed, like leather and liquor, gold was neither expensive nor hard to find in Greece. This privileged domain was off limits for me. My level of trickery was more venial. As a permanent traveler in those convoys, I never spent my pay. Instead, from Belgrade, I would occasionally use the military mail to send my parents cartons of cigarettes, which they swapped for meat.

Then came July 20, 1944: in Rastenburg, Count Claus Schenk von Stauffenberg tried to assassinate Hitler. The propaganda was frenzied: someone wanted to kill the Führer; the affront had to be dealt with. Our mission was brutally cut short. I was transferred to a Berlin barracks. Once again with no specialty, I was given crash courses by vociferous and reckless junior officers, all of them displaying a ferocious zeal.

The terror was complete. The Allied bombings doubled their strength; the leaflets rained down on us. But the majority of Berliners, a stoic breed, seemed to have more confidence than ever in their leader. Squatting in underground military structures, we had to help the civilians, who, like us, had endured forty consecutive days of round-the-clock bombings. Forty days in our hole, which was connected to the subway. Forty days without a glimpse of sunlight, while scenes of panic unfolded in the subway tunnels. The dead and the wounded had to be evacuated. Women gave birth on the ground.

Terrified by these scenes of horror, I behaved like a robot. In that subterranean hell, I felt immensely alone. On the verge of turning twenty-one, how could I have quelled my mental confusion, my urge to die? Today I am still haunted by the roar of the bombers, their muffled deflagrations, and that brief hush between the detonation and the shrieks.

The dream of the great Reich was crumbling everywhere. Hitler had lost the Battle of Stalingrad, the Allies were in Rome, D-Day had just taken place with a decisive breakthrough in Avranches, and French general Jean-Marie-Gabriel de Lattre de Tassigny was about to land in Provence. Paris would soon be liberated. In the chaos that was starting to become ubiquitous, a semblance of a company was formed. I would now be sent to the Russian front, because the Soviet offensive was still on the eastern bank of the Vistula.

That was our destination. On the eastbound train, we sat mute, realizing we were headed toward the final slaughter. To our left, we saw Warsaw ablaze. Then we reached Smolensk: the Russians had shoved the Germans back this far, putting 120 miles between them and Moscow. I couldn't spot the front lines right away, but the incessant booming of the cannons sounded very close. The dreadful efficiency of Stalin's cannons terrified us. Stuck to the frozen ground, we heard the trajectories of the shells and tried to assess whether we were in danger. That din still haunts me today. We replaced exhausted troops who lived buried in glacial trenches. My overriding memory of that horrible winter of 1944 is obsessive hunger—a hunger so intense that we ripped chunks of meat from dead horses and ate them raw.

Again, I became an officer's orderly. One day, his horse, panicked by a nearby detonation, reared and bolted. As punishment, they sent me and another Alsatian of my age, with a machine gun, to an advanced position on a tiny island in the Vistula. Landing there after crossing an unfrozen arm of the river, we were dangerously exposed. And indeed, the Russians, across from us, caught on to our nocturnal stratagem and peppered us with bullets. We were unable to shoot back. That would have given away our position. Any respite only let us catch our breath as we waited for a new attack. Our being Alsatians put us in the worst predicament—we were paralyzed and powerless. What were we doing there, with the Russians ahead of us and the Germans behind us, on the other side of the water?

During the next round of machine-gunning, my comrade, a blond, well-built guy, was killed at my side. I took him by the shoulders, I shook him, I talked to him, I hugged him. And I lived for three days and three nights, standing in our hole, with that dead man next to me. We no longer had telegraph facilities. On the German shore, there was no sign that anyone was going to rescue me, or even knew of my existence. Eventually I began yelling. My life was at stake. In the evening, the Germans cautiously disembarked and looked for me. My comrade remained in the hole. After three days, he was starting to ice over, frozen in his final position. That proximity of death, those three days next to the corpse, left me with an inexpressible attachment. By now I have forgotten the name of that friend who was killed at my side, but I recall his features as if I had seen them just yesterday.

I had taken his papers. After the Liberation, I visited his parents in Strasbourg. His father received me. Deeply moved, he served me a schnapps. I wanted to tell him about his son's final moments. I felt it was my duty, even if it revived past sufferings and reopened wounds. Survivors like to hear about the dead. But I was almost sorry I had come, for his mother had lost her mind. She kept touching me, shaking me: "You saw him dead? Then it was you who killed him!" The father, confused and crushed, gently saw me out and thanked me.

I was reassigned to my officer. He was young but heavily decorated. Once again we were worming our way over frozen soil. The nights were dreadful; I saw shadows stirring everywhere. The Russians were a lot more familiar with this icy ground and these moonless nights than the Germans were. I was afraid of being jerked awake and seeing my killer before I could do anything: the cold makes you sleepy, and it's a profound and very dangerous sleep.

One evening, when I was returning after a tour of the encampments to transmit my officer's final orders, I entered our shelter—and caught him listening to the BBC.

"But Herr Lieutenant, that's illegal! We're going to get into trouble!"

"Shut up! We have to keep informed. I must tell you, the situation is desperate. This is the right moment to flee."

And indeed, the German army was on the verge of collapse. Standing at attention, I was dumbstruck, my mind abuzz with a thousand different thoughts.

He added, "You'll be leaving with me. After all, we're both Rhinelanders. We'll go home, I to Cologne and you to Strasbourg. Hurry up, pack some light bags. Okay?"

I felt I'd be running out on my Alsatian comrades, who would soon be mowed down by the Russian offensive, and that I'd be deserting with this German officer. But I agreed. I packed some makeshift food while he pocketed a compass and bullets for our revolvers.

We managed to leave the front line without being noticed. "If either of us dies, the other will take his papers and notify his family," he had said. Even though he always used a commanding tone with me, I respected him. By sharing the same extreme risks, we had developed a sort of bond. For me it was a great chance: everything had happened very fast, and I hadn't given it much thought before deserting. In the end, it was really the only solution. On the other hand, we underestimated the distance from the Vistula to the Rhine: twelve hundred miles.

We traveled only at night, digging in during the day. The officer's prediction looked accurate. The tanks we soon heard on the roads were indeed Russian. The Germans, in small groups that were encircled one after the other, did not hold out for long. The Russians executed most of them on the spot to avoid slowing the progress of the conquering troops. On the third day of our own advance toward the west, I was certain that all my comrades who had been forced into the Wehrmacht were dead.

The panzers on those precarious roads were preventively machine-gunning all around, like hunters flushing out game. Did my fellow deserter stick his head out prematurely from our hiding place? A blind volley blasted him right in the chest. He fell back into the underbrush. As he lay dying at my side, I remained immobile. The panzer column apparently noticed nothing: they fired no additional shots. For an instant the shaking ground made me think a tank was lumbering straight toward me. When the danger was past, I bade farewell to my dead comrade; I took his papers and his compass. Then, unable to bury him, I covered his body with a shallow layer of snow.

Though alone, I felt strong and resolute. I waited until nightfall to continue along my deadly route. I was in a forest of birches. Checking the stars whenever I could, I kept trudging west until I was exhausted. I wanted to get as far away as possible from those tragic places. In an isolated clearing in the heart of the forest, I spotted a forester's cottage. I heard abandoned cattle bellowing in the adjoining stable—a sign of the recent massacre or sudden departure of the inhabitants; the chimney was still smoking. I entered. No noise. I lit some matches to see in the dark. I found a large hallway, a yellowed map on the wall, and clothes hanging on pegs. I also found some food—bread crusts, horrible curdled milk, and a churn ready to yield butter. Risking discovery, I stoked the fire.

What was to become of me? To survive in this new situation, I had to change my identity yet again. What was

I? Alsatian? French? German? Was I a traitor? A deportee? A POW? A deserter? For the moment I was a man
trying to escape the bullets of a conflict in which I had
no place. Like any hunted animal, I didn't stop to think.
I instinctively undressed and burned the uniform and
the German documents, including my comrade's after
memorizing his name and address. My survival was at
stake. All I kept was my mother's black rosary and a couple of family photographs. From now on, if I met
Germans I'd be a German trying to escape the Russian
offensive, and if I met Russians I'd be a Frenchman
escaping a prison camp, a deportee roaming the Polish
countryside. In that large bed, under a huge eiderdown,
next to a dying fire, absently telling the beads of the
rosary I was already wearing around my neck, I regained
a little serenity.

My sleep was profound. At dawn, the cows bellowed all
the louder. I saw the milk streaming from their udders,
but not being from the country, I didn't know how to
milk them. Besides, I feared getting a bad kick. Inside the
house there was a sewing machine with its oil can. In
front of a mirror I redid my hair, slicking it down with the
oily liquid and reassuming a few silly gestures of coquet-
tishness. I smiled at myself. This wild freedom restored a
bit of my self-esteem. At twilight, I checked out the sur-
roundings. The poor, very flat countryside was swampy,
with birches and ferny underbrush — everything covered
with snow and cold. Almost hugging the wall, I studied

the regional map, on which I located the house and the surrounding roads: a village was not far off. I spent a second night with no problems. But it was impossible to stay on, especially since there was no food left. I slipped back into the forester's civilian clothes and waited for the following night to take the road indicated on the map. I advanced. I spotted smoke from distant cottages. In icy weather, smoke is always thick.

On the outskirts of the village, I made out some armed sentinels in the middle of the road. I heard a shout, "Who's there?" in Russian. At last! I answered from as far away as I could: "Fransooski [French]!" (During my time in Yugoslavia, I had picked up a smattering of Slavic languages.) They didn't shoot, but four or five of them pounced on me. I yielded. They dragged me to a house, where the main room was illuminated by numerous kerosene lamps. In this gathering, where all the men seemed to have drunk a lot, I easily recognized the officer by his boots and stripes, his better appearance, and his lesser degree of sloppiness. They all glared at me, intrigued and distrustful. They seemed to doubt my nationality. My hair was still slicked down with sewing-machine oil. One of them shouted, "Spy!"

Was I a spy? The officer made me strip. They took my watch. Fear surged up from my belly. Someone else cried, "Catholic!" The Orthodox don't have rosaries. They let me dress again. They tried to forge ahead in their collective interrogation, but I couldn't reply without an interpreter. I kept saying, "De Gaulle! Stalin! Communist! France!" At last the gesture I was waiting for came: the officer handed me his glass. I was accepted by them. We drank to France, to Russia. I had to imbibe their elixir: it was something like alcohol mixed with tank gas—a horror that immediately got me drunk. Each toast was less comprehensible than the last. Seeing how skinny I was, they must have concluded that I had escaped from a camp: Treblinka, among others, was not far. They granted me a piece of bread. I was happy: they were my liberators. Suddenly my luck had changed. The night was less silent than the preceding ones, for everybody snored—and they also stank. But that was fine with me.

The next day the men resumed their westward march. They also yelled out their orders, but in a different way from the Germans. I remained within a few feet of the officer, discreetly seeking his protection. For even if my stratagem had paid off, my situation was still precarious. Granted, the canteen was following us and I had almost enough to eat, with some hot drinks every now and then. But I worried being among these drunkards, who, not knowing me, could have easily polished me off with a rifle or revolver. I was still anything but safe.

Spring 1945 was on its way. We pushed from village to village. But to my eyes, the landscapes of war were all alike: forced marches, encirclements, arrests, executions. Each night the best house was assigned to the officers. As we crossed Poland, we got closer and closer to the German border.

One day, we were joined by two female officers. They had brought along a complete radio apparatus. They also spoke a little French. They were educated, and I enjoyed chatting with them whenever the unit halted. One day they let me listen to a French broadcast. That was how I learned the overwhelming news: France had been liberated! In honor of my great happiness, they sewed a small tricolor flag on my blouse. Nazi Germany was being routed, and aside from a few pockets of resistance, the Russians were advancing rapidly. Everyday life had sharply improved, and we now ate brioches, jam, and brandy cherries. We were inundated with alcohol. The whole time I was with the Soviet army, I don't believe I was ever truly sober. In my drunken evenings, gazing at the heavens with dim eyes, I began to dream that having escaped so much horror, my troubles were over and I would soon be returning to Alsace. I was sadly mistaken.

We reached a large village, whose name, if I ever knew it, has long since faded from my mind. It was made up chiefly of large scattered houses. At the crack of dawn, I was awakened by shrieks. Everyone was yelling and dashing about. I understood that a captain had been missing at roll call. He had been sleeping in the house facing mine. They found him lying across his bed, bathed in his own blood, murdered.

Things moved very fast after that. The unit assembled all the villagers on the main square. The men, including a few prisoners in German uniforms, were lined up against the graveyard wall. Still next to my groggy officer, I witnessed an altercation concerning me. A military security officer absolutely insisted that I join the men rounded up: I was as much a suspect as the others. After an angry exchange, my officer buckled. I found myself with my back to the wall amid those young and not so young men.

I had survived torture by the Gestapo, internment at Schirmeck, hand-to-hand combat in Croatia, bombs in Berlin and Greece, machine guns in Smolensk, and roundups by the Russians during my desertion—was I now going to end up so absurdly, under the bullets of the men who had liberated half of Europe? Was I going to die without seeing my family and my country? No one would ever know that on a freezing morning in Poland, a volley of gunfire in reprisal for an officer's assassination had ended my life—a life buffeted by senseless conflicts amid the chaos of a history that had gone insane. The Communists weren't my enemies; they had liberated me from the Nazis. Why would they shoot me?

Who knows what sudden inspiration crossed my mind? Detaching myself from the graveyard wall against which we had been brutally shoved, I stepped forward and intoned the *Internationale*. In the icy dawn wind, my voice did not sound very confident. But across from me,

after all that agitation, I noticed a strange hush border-
ing on stupefaction. Then a certain embarrassment
appeared. Probably last night's liquor and the grief at
losing their comrade had sharpened their desire to get it
over with and massacre the hostages. But the boldness of
this official ally, this Frenchman, with his national colors
on his shoulder, seemed to make them vacillate. Was I to
be hastily mowed down like a common hostage among
others when I was singing their sacred anthem?

After I finished, exhausted, merely humming the
melody of that famous song, since I knew only one
stanza, I saw two officers jointly order the execution
squad to lower its arms. They let me leave the wall. I
dashed toward them, wild with gratitude and incapable
of containing my emotions.

The execution squad shouldered their arms again, and
a dozen hostages lay on the ground, riddled with bullets.
The NCOs now approached the dying to give them the
coup de grâce in the back of their necks. The Russian
officers authorized the rest of the unit to strip the
corpses of any shoes and clothes they liked. Finally, the
women and children were allowed to approach and sob
over their sons, brothers, husbands, and fathers.

In the cemetery the Russians had already dug a hole to
hastily bury their officer, who lay on a simple plank.
Some of the men were crying. I don't recall whether they
fired a salute. However, I do remember that when I
passed close to the corpse, my nerves were so tightly

knotted that I felt an absurd and uncontrollable urge to laugh.

A few days later, after those months of living together, we separated. The Russians had to reach Berlin as fast as they could, for they had to negotiate the most favorable division of Germany with the other Allies. As we know, that was what happened, and Germany was cut in two for almost half a century.

My Russian friends had made a list of the men who were Germans and those who they were sure were not. The former group was taken east to the gulags, from which they never returned. The other group, including myself, trudged on in long, exhausted files, joined by inmates escaping from the death camps. We reached the Polish city of Bitgosh. There we were handed over to the authorities of a camp, where I found a few Frenchmen. We were told that we were going to be repatriated. We were mixed in with the concentration-camp survivors, who were like the living dead. For all the camps had opened their doors, releasing dazed and dying prisoners. The mountains of corpses discovered by our liberators had finally enlightened them about the vast scope of the Nazi horror, the monstrosity of unparalleled crimes.

Even today, I find it hard to overcome my aversion to anything German. I know that it's unfair and hurtful, especially for the younger generation, which cannot be held accountable for the atrocities committed by their parents. But I can't help it: it's inscribed inside me on too deep a level for me to change or control it. Whatever my good will, my emotions are too powerful.

In the repatriation camp, there were only men. We got almost enough to eat. I dreamed about France—a dream still remote when France, though already liberated, was six hundred miles away. I was prudent enough to remain tight-lipped. I was simply happy to be alive.

When the winter of 1944 drew to its end, I started believing that the nightmares were finally behind me. Cautiously, I began looking for familiar faces; I tried to speak Alsatian and even French, which had been prohibited for me since June 1940. I still haven't gotten over that fiat: even today, German, Alsatian, and French compete in my head, interfering with my speech. I still rely on a German-French dictionary.

We finally were taken over by the Red Cross, with which the Allies had reached international agreements. We assumed that our repatriation would take place along the east–west axis. But instead, we traveled along the north–south axis, via Odessa and the Black Sea. Six hundred miles. A convoy was formed. The train began a very drawn-out journey. Sometimes, abandoned by our Russian escort, our train would be stalled for hours on end in some tiny town. A few of the travelers took advantage of these pauses to have sex with some women under a porch. Others tried to find tobacco. For my part, I seldom left the train; I merely stared far away, at the village church. My exhaustion was bottomless.

I recall the eighth of May 1945, V-E Day. The armistice. Peace was finally restored in Europe, after the carnage. We still hadn't left Polish soil. Our convoy was again immobilized in a village, where we roamed the streets. All the bells were pealing. The churches were full, the blessings and hallelujahs succeeded the *Te Deums*. People were kneeling in prayer on the sidewalks. I myself had lost all sense of prayer. Once again, I was starving. All I had left in my pouch was a new toothbrush, as yet unwrapped. In the marketplace I managed to swap it for a piece of bread. I was only twenty-two years old and I can still feel my anger. Forgive? At most, forgiveness for those who asked for it. But the others?

We finally reached Odessa in a railroad car containing "40 men — 8 horses." The heat of that summer of 1945 was devastating to our frail, sickly frames. Many of us died, chiefly of typhus. We jettisoned the corpses whenever we crossed a river. Arriving safely at last, we couldn't get into the sanatorium, which was crowded and fairly dilapidated. Tents, according to nationality, were pitched on the beach. Each group chose a nearby tree for nailing messages, information regarding searches, and appointments. We felt an irresistible urge to communicate after all that sound and fury. We needed to find one another and talk amid those drifting human masses.

That was how I came upon the pharmacist from the rue du Sauvage, Mulhouse; he had escaped from a camp. More precisely, it was he who recognized me, for I suffered from an agonizing amnesia. He convinced me that I was indeed the son of Seel, the owner of the pastry shop. I showed him my family photos. He commented on them. A traveler without baggage, I thus regained a few shreds of my demolished identity.

Finally, thanks to the Red Cross, I could let my parents know I was alive: they hadn't heard from me in eight months, since the Battle of Smolensk. Notifying them was something, at least, even though I could receive no news of them or of my brothers and my sister.

There were a few clergymen in lay clothing among us; they had escaped from the camps. Underneath a tree, sheltered from prying glances, they would consecrate the hosts, and we would celebrate Mass. Next to me stood a friend from Tarn. Our Masses were clandestine because, like our former oppressors, the people working on our repatriation were ideologically hostile to all churches. So we had to be as discreet as possible. Those moments of communion enabled us to patiently endure our woes and to fervently look forward to the homecoming that we so greatly desired.

Since I was the smallest and most retiring person, I don't know why the authorities designated me to keep order in that encampment. I had to settle unavoidable quarrels and help maintain collective hygiene, for malaria had made a disquieting appearance among us. Terrified by my mission, I appealed to everyone's common sense and overall solidarity: "Be reasonable. In a few days, we'll be home. We've survived the horror, so let's make things as easy as possible. Let's agree on a collective discipline." It seemed to work fairly well. But I too came down with malaria, which still causes me feverish nights and keeps me bedridden for days at a time.

However, might tried to make right, of course—in the person of a man from Toulouse. One evening, during an obligatory inspection, I admonished him, "Do what everyone else does: take your mess bowl, go to the water, scrub your bowl, rinse it, and dry it." He gaped at me, motionless, silent, his eyes locking with mine in front of everyone. So I took his bowl and hurled it far out into the sea. He gave me a look full of hatred. But he sensed that the others were on my side and so he finally backed down.

A few days later, some physicians and officers came to inspect us. They were Frenchmen, who had flown in from Paris. Deeply moved, I told them a little about my adventures. They replied, "You are now under the protection of France. Say nothing. Your name is Celle, and you are a native of Delles in the territory of Belfort." I had to hide the fact that I was Alsatian! More camouflage, more half-truths, more forced secrecy.

Under the pretext of a medical inspection, the Red Cross doctors, aided by officers, examined the occupants of my tent, making them strip to the waist and hold up their arms. That was how they discovered the members of the League of French Volunteers—Frenchmen who had willingly joined the German army. Each had his blood type tattooed under one arm, in case he blacked out after being wounded and needed a transfusion. They were instantly arrested.

Thus, even in this camp at the end of the world, ready to find freedom again after our calvary, we were still living with our enemies? What were they? Bastards or dupes fascinated by Nazism and its hateful ideology? I cannot answer. In any case, that very evening, a huge number of them were flown back to French soil to be incarcerated and quickly tried. The man from Toulouse, who had regularly defied me, was part of that group.

I also experienced moments of astonishment, or rather adoration, in the presence of a young man whom I perhaps could have met up with later had I wanted to. He frequently meditated, isolating himself under a ledge, where I would often go walking in my boredom. The son of the Norwegian ambassador to France, he had been deported with his family. We often swam together, effortlessly buoyed up for a long time on the surface of the very salty Black Sea. He was quite uncomfortable with his beauty, which drew everyone's attention. He was seeking God, calling Him here at twilight. Did he believe in Him? He said God was a reference for him, something to go by, an urgent appointment with himself whenever he was unhappy.

We thus got together every evening, but our discussions were awkward because of his poor French. We talked about the values of life and often conjured up our reunions with our families. We told each other that after years of being ordered around in a closed authoritarian universe, where everything was programmed, we were about to regain the strength of our free choice, our commitments and responsibilities. We were frightened, for we had forgotten how to deal with those situations. Long silences punctuated our conversations. I have never found another man of such noble beauty.

The lend-lease contract had been operating for years. With the start of the Russian offensive, Great Britain had provided material assistance to the Soviets. This support had been extended to all the anti-Axis powers, then had been made official by the United States. A law initiated by Roosevelt had been passed in March 1941. In the summer of 1945, on the shores of the Black Sea, that law was translated into convoys of food for Odessa as well as weapons, airplanes, and spare parts, for world peace had not been attained as yet—the Japanese were still holding out. When those convoys headed back, they took along contingents of West European prisoners. French General Marie-Pierre-Joseph-François Koenig came to visit us, while de Gaulle, who truly cared about our long, painful exile, was received by Stalin in pomp and circumstance. We waited for our repatriation with growing impatience. But the embarkments by sea were few and far between, the docks were crowded and the waiting was interminable. To help us exercise patience, they made us practice embarking with identity cords around our necks.

One day, yet again, I found myself on the dock with the cord around my neck indicating that I was Pierre Celle from Belfort. At the last minute, however, an officer came running up, gave some counterorders, and several of us were removed from the ship that was sailing to Marseilles via Sardinia. Priority was being given to a few women, who walked past us and took our places. Some were pregnant and had probably been raped by the occupiers. But others, who seemed more withdrawn, would probably have their heads shaved upon arriving—the punishment inflicted on Frenchwomen who had consorted with the enemy. We were so furious that in the evening we sang terribly misogynist songs in our encampment. A few men chanted, "Women overboard!"

Later we learned that the ship had struck a mine and blown up in the Dardanelles: there were no survivors. The authorities had notified my parents that I would be sailing on that ship, and when they read the newspapers they believed that I had tragically perished at sea.

Meanwhile lend-lease was terminated, and we were still waiting. First it was a rumor, then a certainty: there was no ship for us. I was all the more frightened because the encampment was filled with mutterings of anger and revolt. Then we were informed that we would be repatriated all the same, but in the other direction: by rail through Rumania, Germany, Holland, and Belgium.

Again six hundred miles, but by the opposite route.

And that was what happened. I remember that the Dutch offered us apples, and that we then received a liter of red wine in Blanc-Misseron, at the French border. The closer we got to our beloved French capital, the more strictly we were checked. New arrests of collaborators were made right in front of us. And more people died along the way.

At last, we reached Paris. I cannot describe my emotions when I set foot on Parisian soil. That seventh of August 1945 we were directed to the Lycée Michelet to show our papers and set up medical files. I was handed a repatriation card. I could telephone my dear Parisian godmother, who thought I had drowned in the Dardanelles. The authorities allowed me to spend my first evening in France at her home. I called up my parents, who likewise had thought I was dead. I said I would join them before long and hold them in my arms.

When I returned to the Lycée Michelet the next morning, I was told I would be leaving for Chalons-sur-Saône, where a special checkpoint had been set up to investigate the Alsatians and Lorrainers one last time and sort out the final collaborators or Germans with false papers. The Liberation authorities had impressive lists of names and were tightening their nets around fugitives who had infiltrated the final convoys.

But secretaries were needed to register those human masses, and I was drafted, along with others. In despair,

I had to check off the homeward bound while I remained there, drudging behind a desk. All I wanted was to end my four years of exile, but I continued to molder away in that office, itemizing escapees, their faces beaming at the thought of reuniting with their families. France had been free for a year now. Every evening, I telephoned my parents on the military lines: "I'm coming! I'm coming!" But they were not reassured: "Why are they holding you back? You aren't charged with anything!"

I was finally one of the very last to reach Alsace. The press was waiting for us at the Mulhouse station. I answered their questions very tersely. For I did not dare reveal everything about myself. I was already starting to censor my memories, and I realized that despite my expectations, despite all the things I had imagined, despite the emotions of my homecoming, which I had looked forward to for such a long time—despite all that, Liberation was only for others.

Chapter 4
Years of Shame

How immense was my joy when I was finally reunited with my family. After the four years described in the preceding chapters, we celebrated both my homecoming and my twenty-second birthday. But my body was exhausted from too many ordeals and my mind ravaged by too many horrors.

My family had likewise changed. Except for the eldest, all my brothers were back from the war and nearly all of them had wives. One had married in a German military hospital. He had been taken prisoner in 1940, at the battle of Amiens, during the blitzkrieg; he was seriously wounded by a detonating bullet. Another of my brothers had visited his hospital in the Rhineland several times, donating blood to him.

As for my sister, she had left in 1942 with the RAD of Alsatian women, which followed the men's RAD for several months. She had worked in German territory, first on a farm, to replace the men, who were mobilized, then in a factory for precision parts, where she was liberated by the advancing Allied forces. Some of her friends had spent months in underground passages on the other side of the Rhine. For a long time, my sister had to wear dark glasses because her eyes couldn't stand the light of day.

The wife of one of my brothers had been denounced and arrested for helping resisters and Allied aviators across the Vosges. Together with her father and her sister, she had been incarcerated in the Mulhouse city jail. She was tortured by the Gestapo and, among other agonies, had to suffer that of the tub. She was also interned for six months in the Gaggenau concentration camp, on the other side of the Rhine, until the French army liberated her and all her fellow inmates.

My eldest brother was the last to return—two weeks after me. He was a passionate musician, an organist who had studied with Albert Schweitzer. At home, he had always dreamed of our forming a quartet. As a POW in the camp at Tambov, he had organized musical training. In short, by some miracle, we were all reunited.

I had come back from hell. I had been deprived of everything and endured immense tortures. I was happy being with my family, who feted the youngest son for dodging death and escaping Europe's carnage, but my greatest delight was finding my bed again. I wanted to sleep for days, weeks, and months, in order to put a huge mental gap between myself and my wounds.

I returned as a ghost; I remained a ghost: it probably didn't fully hit me that I was still alive. Nightmares haunted me day and night; I practiced silence. I wanted to forget all the details and all the terrors of those four years that I had lived through. I was totally exhausted by my multiple encounters with death, and I painfully realized how powerless I had been in regard to the deaths of other people. A huge sadness took hold of me. And I felt no desire.

Outside, the Liberation, with all its accompanying exuberance, had made homosexuality more visible in Mulhouse. The same thing was happening in certain neighborhoods of big cities, like Saint-Germain-des-Prés in Paris. In my town, the grand-bourgeois homosexuals had all returned. They appeared not to have suffered under the occupation. They talked about nothing; they made no statements. There was no public discussion about what had happened to homosexuals. Nothing came to rescue me from my silence.

I decided I would break totally with the intimate parties that had resumed at the café concert. I was incensed, for even if these men had not been interrogated by the Gestapo, they must have noticed that some of their acquaintances had vanished. They may not have lived behind the barbed wire of a camp, but they had heard about the roundups of homosexuals in Alsace. They may not have been forced to watch the massacre of a friend, but they must have at least been told that for four years homosexuals had been branded undesirables on that occupied soil and that they had been tortured, expelled, and even murdered. The police lists, updated year after year before the arrival of the Nazis, and the denunciations during the occupation had done their work for hundreds of us.

Granted, Alsace was liberated and once again under French jurisdiction. But meanwhile the Pétain government, at Admiral Darlan's behest, had adopted an anti-homosexual law, the first in 150 years—indeed, the first since the Old Regime. At the Liberation, de Gaulle's government had implemented a highly approximate cleansing of the French penal code. But while the shameful anti-Semitic laws disappeared, the anti-homosexual law survived. It took pitched battles to wipe that law off the books forty years later, in 1981.

Upon hearing about that law, I understood that by speaking out, I risked being put on trial or accused of apologizing for "unnatural" sexuality. This judicial status may have explained the silence of the middle-class homosexuals in Mulhouse. But their silence struck me as different from mine. So I stayed clear of them. As for cruising the squares, they had become very dangerous because the nocturnal violence had escalated. What was the source of that new hatred of homosexuals? Perhaps it was caused by the Frenchmen who were angry about the

Allied victory. Drunk on beer, they would scour Mulhouse in the dead of night and, like hooligans and black-
mailing hustlers, they found ready-made victims. So I
kept to myself.

To ease my daily malaise and to avoid dealing with my
own life, I devoted myself to others. The war had left
Alsace with severe shortages, which affected the most
deprived people. Together with a cousin on my mother's
side, I founded an association for helping the victims in
Mulhouse; this was a section of the Society of War
Victims and Other Victims in Alsace. With the help of a
list my cousin got from the social services, I contacted
certain impoverished families, whom I supplied with
clothing, condensed milk, and coffee. Three times a
week for three years, crates piled up in the hallways of
our home, and those families would come by for these
donations.

I did this in my spare time or right after work, for I'd
had to find a job immediately. I found myself in the garment business, but once again at the bottom of the lad-
der. As inventory manager, I worked in warehouses
across from the Mulhouse railroad station. In 1944, this
district had suffered intense Allied air raids, which had
killed hundreds of people. We now walked on planks or
waded in water that seeped in through the yawning holes
left by the bombs.

Upon my return from the Schirmeck camp, my father
had imposed a pact of silence about my homosexuality,

and that law persisted in our home: no revelations from me, no questions from them. We all acted as if nothing had happened. But my homosexual label was known to the entire family. My "reintegration" into the family embarrassed the most bigoted relatives and those most concerned about our public image.

I remember an incident during those early postwar years: At a family gathering, one guest, sitting opposite me, cracked some jokes about homosexuals. I told my parents that it was time to leave. During that same period I suffered another humiliation: when my godfather died, I was publicly informed that I needn't bother seeing his lawyer since, for obvious reasons, I was not mentioned in his will.

I thus lived through four years of solitude, surrounded by whispers. My job and the association for impoverished war victims took up most of my time. Beyond that, I was surrounded by a great silence made up of painful sadness and invisible renunciation. Our house had emptied. My brothers had stayed only briefly between their return from the war and their marriages. My father, growing less and less talkative, had chosen to be mostly pensive and aloof.

I drew closer to my mother. Eight years my father's senior, she had been forty-four at my birth. He had been very depressive, and that final baby had brought new happiness to the couple. My brothers claim that I was my mother's pet. My parents indeed paid special attention to me, often taking my side when I argued with my older brothers.

With the Liberation, my mother saw all her children return after escaping the Nazis, the bullets on all the fronts, and the barbed wire of all the camps. But her daily anxiety had left her in a frail state, with a heart condition that was diagnosed a short time later. She spent many days in bed, and the doctors were getting more and more guarded.

Some afternoons, my brothers would bring her champagne and their wives would bring her flowers. Between visits, she told her rosary. Despite the exhaustion that caused her sufferings, she insisted on remaining stylish. She had her hair done regularly by the housekeeper and wore lipstick and makeup. But she soon required a permanent attendant. In the evening, after the nurse left, I fed my mother and took care of her medicines. Every night I slept in a twin bed in her room. She said she was very happy about our new intimacy. But often the pains grew worse when she was asleep, suffocating her and making her sigh for hours on end.

In 1948, when I turned twenty-five, my mother's condition deteriorated. Our family doctor found serious complications and, worst of all, a spreading cancer. Thus, as she approached death, my every communication with her grew more and more intense. Sometimes she lamented that I was her only son who hadn't married. "My great sorrow," she said, "is that you're going to remain alone with your father." But that was all she said, and she never enjoined me to marry at any price.

Several weeks passed. I had very little time between working and taking care of my mother. Nevertheless I had managed to establish a relationship with a young man of my age. We lived in the same neighborhood, each of us with his parents. We got together regularly but, being very discreet, our relationship could not blossom and provide me with true happiness: that fragile arrangement could not develop into a lifetime companionship. After several months, he told me he was getting married, so we would have to stop seeing each other.

My mother was the only family member who sometimes tried to get me to confide in her, to break my silence and ease my sadness. What had they done to me in Schirmeck that I should come back so crushed, so taciturn, so changed? I seemed to be dragging myself about without regaining any pleasure in life. Why wouldn't I talk to her? She swore that she wouldn't say anything to anyone. But on each occasion, I turned my back on her to hide the tears welling from my eyes, and I placed my hands over my mouth, resisting the temptation to respond.

One evening, when I had just switched off the lamp and said good night, she reached over to my bed and, slipping her fingers between the sheets, she squeezed my shoulder and said, "Pierre, tell me what happened. I want to hear about your sufferings. You know I don't have

much time left. Pierre, don't keep your secret to yourself—talk to me. Tell me what they did to you."

I silently switched the light back on. I no longer know
why and I don't recall what words I used, but I finally
opened up to her completely. I told her about everything
I have described here: my homosexuality, this difference
that made it so hard to live in a family like mine, in a city
like Mulhouse. I told her about how I met my friend Jo.
Then I came to May 1941, the roundup and the tortures at
the hands of the Gestapo. And finally, I told her about
Jo's savage murder, then those long months of horror in
the camp at Schirmeck.

She clearly remembered that evening at the cash register in the pastry shop when, as I was wolfing down
chocolate eclairs after work, she had to tell me, very
nervously, that the Gestapo was ordering me to report
the next morning. She reminded me that she didn't see
me again until six months later—starving and shat-
tered. She asked who could have turned me in to the
Gestapo. She had wondered about my classmate who
had become a Hitler Youth several weeks after the
German invasion.

I replied that it didn't seem likely. To my mind, there
could be only one person: the French police officer who
had processed my complaint about the theft of my watch
one year earlier. Not content with making me sign that
document before reprimanding me, he had added the
name of my teenage self to the list of the city's homosex-

uals. For later on, during the torture session, it was that document that the Gestapo had shown me to make me admit my homosexuality.

My mother was flabbergasted. She knew the French police officer personally. "Him?" she exclaimed. "But we always gave him cakes and candy at Christmas! Remember? So that he wouldn't ticket us so often for a dirty sidewalk outside the shop!"

Indeed, for a long time he had been assigned to checking the downtown sidewalks. The stores were responsible for keeping them clean, and the neighboring stores proceeded as we did to temper that policeman's zeal and abuse. He had been one of the officials who kept the illegal list of homosexuals in that region with the same good conscience as when he ticketed store owners for neglecting dog turds on their sidewalks.

In short, I told her everything. She listened to everything. And I can attest that my secrets were well guarded. It was our intimacy as well as her tact and gentleness that made me want to open up. A barrier had fallen. She was the exception to my pact of silence. It then took me another thirty years to speak again. Back then, she was the only person I could have told; for a long time, I simply couldn't imagine confiding in anyone else. I was utterly convinced that there are things you only tell your mother. I am still deeply moved by the thought of that privileged moment, which was repeated, that complicity, which allowed us to exchange confidences, hopes, sorrows, and memories many times afterward.

I also told her about my recent relationship, but I presented it as a ludicrous hope for happiness, since Jo was still in my heart, and I was haunted by his unpunished murder, which I was not allowed to speak of. She would call me back to the present when, lingering at her bedside, I forgot about my date with my new friend. For he would sometimes grow impatient and whistle discreetly. She'd hear him before I would, spellbound as I was by our serious and profound communication. She would interrupt me, saying, "Go on, your friend's waiting." I would head down almost reluctantly, knowing that my mother had no hope of recovery. At times, I even refused to leave her, preferring to continue our tête-à-tête. Growing weaker and weaker, she would tragically repeat, "I have to go; I'm suffering too much. Please pray to heaven with me; pray for me to die." Although she was lucid, I protested with tears in my eyes.

We could also smile from time to time. One memory that amused us was of a day in my childhood when we were staying in the same hotel as Queen Wilhelmina of Holland, and I jumped into her lap—to her great embarrassment. We also looked back fondly to that glorious day in my adolescence when the two of us ceremoniously opened the ball that ended the festivities of the Union of Pastry Chefs and Confectioners, which was meeting in Mulhouse. That soiree may have seemed ordinary to the guests, but for my mother and me it virtually sealed our relationship of trust and complicity.

Were my trust and openness with her enhanced by my homosexuality? I think so. She likewise confided in me from time to time. It was not just a dialogue between mother and son, much less an exchange between a man and a woman. We shared a similar sensitivity; we felt the same way about people and the world. Moreover, she was about to die: there was no time for camouflage. I was overwhelmed by that threat to our love, and I owed it to myself to tell her everything.

It was the sixth of June 1949. France was preparing to celebrate the fifth anniversary of D-Day, "Operation Overlord"—the victorious landing of the Allies on the coast of Normandy. The rue du Sauvage was already bustling with official festivities. My mother woke me up, saying, "I'm about to die. Put me in my armchair." I jumped out of bed and placed her in the armchair. Without a word, I hugged her tightly. "Make me a good coffee," she murmured. She drank the coffee down to the silver filter, which I have piously preserved. Then she died in my arms.

My anguish was immeasurable. The death of the woman who had given birth to me brought a sorrow that was unutterable, incommunicable. The imminence of her death may have enabled me to confide in her, empowered me to boldly verbalize things that were never spoken of in a family as conventional as ours. Death sealed my confessions. When she died, she took with her the memory of my incarceration in the camp, my homosexuality, Jo's murder. My life was now cut in two, and my memory was buried with my mother, who had made it possible for me to open up.

According to Alsatian tradition, the chief mourners for a dead mother are her husband and her unmarried children. I therefore had to bear the brunt of the grief with my father, who did not survive her for long. All eyes were upon me when I, with my pale skin, placed an armful of red roses on the coffin, which then sank into the ground. Then I burst into sobs. They led me away. My aunt splashed water in my face, and two doctors gave me an injection to calm me down. No one understood that unleashing of immense despair. Who could guess that my mother had died with all my secrets? That she was their sole depository? Bereft of my mother, I lived on, definitively alone.

The house now had to be reorganized. I quickly realized that she had indeed run everything during her lifetime. I was left alone with my father. Evenings, after work, we barely spoke, sharing our grief amid everyday actions in an atmosphere of utter desolation. Soon my poor father was felled by a stroke, which paralyzed his left side. It happened one evening when we were dining silently, face to face: the spoon he was bringing to his lips suddenly dropped from his hand. From then on I had to feed him every evening and put him to bed. Madame Berthe, the housekeeper, helped me as much as possible, and so did other women in the family. But everyone saw that I was at the end of my tether. At a family council, we decided to find my father a place where he would be better cared for. His sister Séraphica, the nun, found a nursing home, where his room, complete with furniture, could be replicated. He died on November 6, 1954, at the age of sixty-seven, thirteen years to the day after my release from Schirmeck. He maintained his total silence about my homosexuality until the very end: it never came up between us.

Little by little, I became convinced that it would be impossible for me to live as a homosexual. Even though I'd been liberated from the Nazi yoke, I could not resume my prewar existence. I was repelled by the thought of living like the bourgeois homosexuals of Mulhouse or the frightened shadows on the squares. No doubt, I was equally paralyzed by my concern for preserving my family's reputation in our city. In fact, one of my brothers had become a deputy-mayor. So I began eradicating my homosexuality from my life. How could I hope to succeed? Homosexual experience is indelible, and sooner or later a man who has had even one experience will seek more.

Because of my mother's illness, our family get-togethers had taken place at the homes of my brothers or their parents-in-law. I was always placed next to a young woman, either a brother's sister-in-law, a friend of one of the couples, or a tennis partner. But it made me feel all the icier the more I sensed the ulterior motive behind so much attention. I started dreaming about an entirely different kind of life—I wanted to be free of all those inquisitive glances from around the table or out in the street.

I longed to have my own home, to get my life on an honorable course. These wishes allowed me to pursue a legitimate goal: I wanted to have children some day, and grandchildren. It was thus that I made my strange decision to get married. Perhaps children could reconcile me with the loss of my youth and with life. I was only twenty-six, and yet I felt very old.

I was certain I would have to meet my future spouse far from Mulhouse and its harmful rumors. I found the address of a marriage bureau in Paris. I wrote a letter, enclosing my photo and my references. The young woman would have to be Catholic, for I feared that a "mixed" marriage would make the situation even more complicated. Ultimately, I was resorting to the same method my parents had used to find each other. A short time later, I received a photo of a pretty young woman who suggested that we meet.

We got together in Paris, at the Café Notre-Dame on the other side of the cathedral. She wore a small veil, was pretty, and I liked her. Very soon she offered to introduce me to her parents, who lived in Saint-Ouen. During the introduction dinner, I experienced the Iberian rite of the orange: the prospective parents-in-law offer you this fruit as a sign of commitment, and you have to eat it by slicing it according to the rules. In Slavic countries, you are offered a plate of salt, and you take a pinch.

She was the daughter of a Spanish refugee who had immigrated to France; an atheist and anarchist, he had been sentenced to death in his country. Throughout her teens, his daughter had suffered nationalistic teasing from her classmates. One day, the teacher called her a "dirty spick," and the girl threw an inkwell in her face. A disciplinary hearing was held, but since she was a brilliant student, she was not expelled. Eventually she got a degree in law. When he was on his deathbed, her father, a man of great warmth and great authenticity, would make all his children swear never to set foot on Spanish soil while Franco remained in power.

She and I still hadn't kissed or started using the familiar form. After the introduction, I spent the night at the home of my Parisian godmother. The next day I went back to Mulhouse. En route, I caught myself thinking that a future could thus open to me, that something was within reach. Tomorrow was no longer blocked off.

Things moved quickly after that. The engagement was celebrated at my godmother's home. And on August 21, 1950, my brother, the deputy-mayor, performed the civil marriage ceremony at the Mulhouse city hall. Then we went to the notary. We had to hurry, for my bride, a school administrator, had asked to be transferred to Mulhouse in the fall. Just one month later, on September

3o, the religious wedding took place at the church of Notre-Dame-du-Rosaire in Saint-Ouen.

Everything looked fine. But why did we settle in Mulhouse? And in my family home to boot? Looking back, I feel it was a big mistake, for not only was I stuck behind my childhood walls, but we also slept in the room where my mother had died. Today I am convinced that we should have set up housekeeping far from Alsace — just the two of us. It would certainly have made my wife happier.

My brothers often invited us to large parties. We also let ourselves be taken to balls. I noticed that my wife was particularly annoyed by the Alsatian dialect. We all used it to underscore our identity and our regained freedom after the Nazi fiats, but it only increased my wife's sense of isolation, unintentionally making her feel like an outsider. French was spoken mainly by intellectuals and burghers, priests and doctors. The city fathers had realized how dangerous that linguistic division could be. They had even launched a poster campaign with the slogan "Speak French, it's chic!" But Alsace dug in its heels. On the spur of the moment, we would run off and spend the day in Belfort for the mere pleasure of hearing French, of enjoying a few hours without being linguistically assaulted on the trolley, at work, or in department stores. Besides, we preferred finding a remote and more intimate ambiance, with fewer friends and relatives.

Something else preyed on my mind: the closeness and

solidarity of the women in my family. Weren't they a
threat to me? Except for my wife, they all knew why I had
been sent to a camp. But *I* couldn't speak, I didn't speak;
hence, I couldn't defend myself against rumors. I clung
ferociously to my secret—keeping it first and foremost
from my wife. Should I have told her? It wasn't until later
that, realizing the scope of the disaster, I reproached
myself for lacking the courage to open up earlier and
reveal all the facts.

Very soon, a baby was on the way. But things turned
bad. Unexpectedly, my wife had to be hospitalized in
Colmar, and she reemerged without the child, which was
stillborn. I had to get rid of the cradle and all the gifts
awaiting the baby. We suffered through the pain of
mourning. That was the first time we truly felt despair. I
was very worried, for our marriage remained very fragile.
We both wanted to become parents and build a home
and family as a haven from outside attacks, but fate did
not ease our task.

In the summer of 1952, two years after our wedding, my
wife was expecting again. However, my father-in-law died
during that period. At the funeral in Paris, my wife suffered a severe hemorrhage. We had to dash back to
Alsace on a medical-emergency train, on which we benefited from a private compartment. Four or five doctors
on the train, who were summoned by loudspeaker,
spelled one another throughout the trip. The baby was
saved, but my wife was bedridden for the remainder of

her pregnancy. As for me, I was finally convinced that it was time the three of us left Alsace. The baby was born in a suburb of Paris. Forty years later, I still refuse to go back to Alsace except for unusual circumstances, even though for these past forty years I have felt like an exile everywhere else.

We settled in the valley of Chevreuse, a rather charming small town one hour from Paris. Here I opened a small textile boutique with a very modest apartment overhead. With my family's approval, I took out a mortgage against my future inheritance. The merchandise, ordered on credit, was meant to appeal to the townsfolk.

We became a real family. A second son was born to us in 1954. Our daughter arrived three years later. We had great moments of happiness. My wife and I agreed to provide a Catholic upbringing for our children, but with no real constraints. We attended Mass every Sunday in a pretty little church, where the entire front row was reserved for a local countess. One year, for the month of Mary, I gave the priest a large amount of blue cloth to decorate the church. We were a well-liked shopkeeping couple.

Being new to this region and having no local ties, my wife and I decided to join a group of young Christian families in the parish; they met on certain evenings to discuss religious, educational, and social problems. In this way, we made contacts beyond Sunday Mass, occasionally spending a Saturday evening with these friends.

Lacking a car and the wherewithal, we could not, as the others did, escape to Paris for a night on the town.

One evening, my wife and I nearly died. I came home late from work. The children were already in their room. My wife told me that she had a horrible headache. We sat down to dinner. I began feeling sluggish; the blood was pounding in my temples. When my wife stood up to get dessert, she reeled, then collapsed. I realized the air was filled with carbon monoxide from the incomplete combustion of coal. I dragged my wife outdoors into the fresh air. We started throwing up violently, but we were saved. The children were out of danger for their room wasn't heated by the coal-burning stove that I had felt it would be sensible to take along from Alsace—an Alsace that was pursuing us with its curse.

Looking back with some detachment, I feel that from the very outset I had a difficult relationship with my children. My daughter, the last-born, seemed farthest away from me, but, to make up for it, she was very close to her mother. However, my malaise concerned chiefly my two sons. They were very handsome. Did I feel I was being spied on? I was worried that somebody would detect some ambiguity in my actions. I didn't know how to express love for them without my gestures being misread. I was paralyzed by an immense timidity. I watched other fathers play with their children, hug them and kiss them. For years on end, I was prey to an ultimately rather absurd terror that my love for them could turn into something else. It was not exactly timidity so much as a sense of embarrassment that prevented me from entering their room or the bathroom when they were inside. My discretion lasted throughout our life together and imperceptibly alienated me from them as they grew up.

Eventually our apartment became cramped and uncomfortable. Our textile shop never got off the ground. Several years later, a stock-market crisis destroyed all the hope we had pinned on our store. Since my wife took care of our children, she no longer worked. I had no choice: given my very narrow professional abilities, the only place I could get a job was Paris.

I found one at Fleuran on the rue Réaumur in the garment district. At its plant in the Vosges, this textile company manufactured table linen as well as complete and very elegant trousseaux. I could hope only for a managerial job, not a top-level position. But I no longer had to stand and face customers; instead I sat behind a desk with a telephone.

I had decided to eradicate homosexuality from my life. But can you stop yourself from thinking? Sometimes I would go to confession, and there I was forced to avow a few solitary pleasures. The priest asked me,

"Whom were you thinking about?"

"A boy."

"Well, then, I can't give you absolution."

"But I can't help it; it's stronger than me."

"I'm sorry."

"But look, I'm a good husband and a responsible father!"

"Sorry. You're in a state of grave sin. There's no absolution."

Emerging from the twilight of those churches into the brightness of the city, with its duties and temptations, I felt even worse than when I had gone in. What good was it? I also met a priest in the parish of the Church of the Trinity; he had written a lot about homosexuality, and I mustered the courage to tell him about being sent to the camp because of my homosexuality. But while he did not condemn my desires, he spoke only about suffering and redemption, which was equally useless. After all those setbacks, I never went to confession again.

Shuttling between the suburbs and Paris was extremely draining and alienated me even more from my family. I would leave, half-asleep, at dawn from the small railroad station and in the evening I would catch the train at Gare Saint-Michel. Some commuters whiled away those hours by playing cards. Others did crossword puzzles. But I remained in my corner, sad and silent, preferring to doze. One evening, the conductor woke me up at the terminal: I was asleep in my seat.

I told myself that despite everything, I had established a home and family and had attained a certain professional dignity. But the thing I never spoke about was there, sticking in my craw like a bone. One day, during a meal with some colleagues, we talked about acquaintances who had been deported; I got up the nerve to say that I too had been in a camp. Instantly, three questions were fired at me: "Where? For what reason? Do you get a pension?" Later on, I was often confronted with those same questions. Since it had not been Auschwitz and since I concealed the reason and did not draw a pension, what little I could say created an uneasiness and I regretted my awkward boldness. I quickly lapsed back into my silence, trying once again to make myself forget.

My wife sometimes got carried away: Why did I refuse to fill out the application for a pension for camp survivors? It would have certainly improved our lives. We could have bought a car to make my commute less exhausting. Our household budget did not permit a very comfortable life. And besides, it would have been only fair. In theory she was right, but she systematically came up against my silent refusals. How could she realize that I would have to reveal the reason for my deportation? Unfortunately she resented my unjustifiable obstinacy.

The secret I clung to likewise interfered with my professional advancement. For there are many homosexuals in the garment and fashion world. Eventually one of them, the top director of a renowned fashion house, offered me a very important position at his side. I hesitated: it was an unexpected windfall that would have meant a better life for my family. Tempted to accept, I decided to consult my wife. But she wouldn't hear of it. Despite the undeniable cachet of that great name in haute couture, his reputation as a homosexual bothered her. Our discussion quickly ended. I put up little resistance, and then I got cold feet. For I sensed that if I didn't give in to her, if I accepted that seductive offer, I might cause a rift between us. And my greatest fear was that I might never see my children again.

A more general malaise took hold of me. Paralyzed by all these contradictions, I felt that our plans for happiness were slowly eluding us, gradually slipping through our fingers. At the beach in the summer, I felt almost disillusioned as I looked at our three children playing on the sand. They were still under ten. At my side, their mother watched them in the distance. She seemed to have given up talking to me, as if an unutterable reproach had created an unbridgeable gap between us. In that holiday sun, I couldn't even put on bathing trunks. The effects of war and incarceration at Schirmeck were too blatant on my legs; the veins had burst like shameful marks that I did not dare expose. I had to remain in trousers like an old man, and yet I hadn't even reached forty.

In the early 1960s I found a job as department head at the Galeries branch in Blois, where we had settled. A waste of time: I was almost immediately transferred to Orléans, where I was put in charge of haberdashery. My daily commuting resumed.

Sales techniques were in the throes of a revolution inspired by the American model; "discount" had just been introduced. I tried to adapt to the new method of orders, which were handled through systems of perforated cards. One day, I punched the wrong box, so that instead of one case of trimmings I ordered a hundred. At the Paris main office, which processed all orders, no one caught the mistake. When I arrived at work in the morning, I couldn't understand what all the strange hubbub was about. An enormous truck was blocking the street, and cases were inundating the stairways and elevators. The staff was either in a state of panic or laughing hysterically. I was thoroughly bawled out by the manager. The surrealistic order had to be siphoned off to all the branches, including the one in Algiers. As for me, I realized I would have to find a new job.

I had to explain to my family that we were about to move again. Through a classified ad, I found work in Compiègne. I didn't try to deceive my future employers about the reasons I had left Orléans. Nevertheless they put me in charge of buying, selling, and statistics. My wife and I were just beginning to benefit—though tardily— from the economic boom of the sixties. At last we had a car and a refrigerator. Then my new bosses sent me to Rouen. Once again, we moved. There was no end in sight, for after a few years they sent me back to Compiègne. This highly unstable period of constant transferring and moving did not help our family life in any way, and it made it hard for us to sustain the friendships we tried to develop in each new place.

My wife had gone back to working in school administration and during vacations she, together with her own children, often accompanied other children to summer camp. In this way I spent many summers alone, feeling bitter and empty. We were back in Compiègne in March 1968 when I suddenly found myself unemployed. Carrefour had just purchased the department store chain I worked for, and large-scale layoffs ensued. I was forty-five years old, my sons were sixteen and fourteen, and my daughter was eleven.

Two months later, the student riots of May '68 exploded. Since I had more free time than other parents, they asked me to go and see what was happening in Paris, where their children were studying. I then had to go to Toulouse because my wife had found an important job there and had asked me to tell her what I thought of the accommodations there.

I drove up to the Sorbonne, which was occupied by students, and I presented myself to the gatekeeper. He distrustfully searched my glove compartment and the trunk. Then he gave the order to open the gate. I thus entered the courtyard of the Sorbonne, which was seething with excitement. The lecture halls were crowded, and whole groups were debating in the stairwells. Some people were sleeping in the classrooms, others were making love unabashedly. I knew that if the police were to storm in, the result would be mayhem. I found one of my nephews at the Maoist booth.

Later on, he was deeply affected by the death of Mao Ze-dong.

I soon felt unnerved: my car was practically requisitioned, and there was no way I could leave. The telephone line was cut, so I couldn't call my wife. Thus I spent three days with these "insurgents" in an atmosphere of smoke and tear gas. We coughed a lot and we often held a handkerchief over our mouths. I attended the discussions in the lecture halls. But a lot of things in those confused ideological debates were over my head. I encountered a world of fervent and generous young people, who were passionate about justice and freedom; but I also recall an immense disorder, a utopian movement faced with massacre. On the fourth day, I succeeded in negotiating my departure.

Greatly relieved, I headed toward Toulouse, where I could check out our future home. But the students in the provinces had risen up after their Parisian colleagues and were storming the streets. On June 12, 1968, trapped between a barricade and a police cordon, I parked on Allées Jean-Jaurès. I stepped out of the car and barely had time to throw myself on the ground, for the police were charging violently. I was picked up and tossed into a prison van, which managed to escape a bunch of students armed with Molotov cocktails. Several hours later, at police headquarters, I was harshly interrogated; for a while, I was under suspicion because of my age: they thought I was an agitator egging on those young rebels.

What was I doing in Toulouse if I lived in Compiègne? Nervous as the police were, I nonetheless convinced them that I was telling the truth, and they released me without incident.

We settled in Toulouse—my wife, my three children, and I—in 1968. Thanks to our new geographic stability, my children succeeded in obtaining their secondary education and then entering prestigious institutions. One of my sons even attended the École Normale in Paris. But the ten years following our move to Toulouse also brought a gradual personal decline to me and the disintegration of our marriage.

I believe that the thing we lacked most was intimacy. I no longer felt at home. I was living in my wife's place. She had accepted a job as "den mother" at the Maison des Compagnons—that is, she headed the entire administration of this austere building, which housed young men apprenticed to very high-level artisans. Traveling around France to perfect their training, the apprentices worked very hard. My wife, who was devoted to her work, had to attend numerous meetings. But actually, I wasn't even living in my wife's "home," we were residing in the Maison des Compagnons. To reach our family's apartment, I had to go through the heavy central door and walk along immense corridors. Everyone could check our comings and goings. I would make my way through austere and silent areas, past countless young trainees, who lived there and, for their part, felt quite at home.

My sole weekly escape came every Friday evening, when I drove to a department store with a shopping list drawn up by my wife, who had also itemized the expenses. Indeed it was she who oversaw our household budget. Although still devoted to my family, I felt I was living in a situation of unrelenting dependence and inferiority. On the way back, I drove through an area that was known as a homosexual cruising ground. I would park under cover of darkness, dreaming as I watched the shadowy game. That life was off limits for me, but how worthwhile was the life I had allowed myself? What could I say about it today other than that it was crushing me? I would return home more silent than ever. A deep depression grew in me, prefiguring my collapse.

Each summer, we went to Alsace to spend a few weeks in the Vosges, at the home of my departed grandparents. But for me the contours of those mountains were depressing. Schirmeck was only a few miles away. At night, unable to sleep, I walked under the trees, recalling my dreadful experiences of the summer of 1941. In 1973, my wife threw a huge party for my fiftieth birthday. I was forced to smile at everyone at that special family celebration. But all at once I felt faint and had to lie down. I was surrounded with embarrassed smiles and reassuring words. But I still held on to my secret, which was silently devouring me like cancer. And I would hold on to it for another eight years.

When we came back from Alsace, my doctor prescribed all sorts of tranquilizers for me, which I swallowed like an addict, but they had no effect other than to keep me permanently on my back. My doctor was a good listener and very attentive—we had actually become friends. But I was unable to tell even him the real reason for my distress. We frequently talked about the deportations, though without my bringing up the reasons for mine. I remember that I very nearly told him. But a mutual constraint existed between us. My condition did not improve.

The Paris headquarters of the Maison des Compagnons offered my wife the position of general director of their house in Toulouse. This would mean attending all the meetings and sharing at least one meal a month with the apprentices. Nervous at the thought of these growing responsibilities, which would further compromise our family life, she consulted me. But I was in no condition to express any opinion. We held a family council and unanimously rejected the offer. My wife was certainly very committed, but this promotion was really something for a widow, an unmarried woman, or the wife of one of the Compagnon members. Acting upon our family decision, she resigned from her job and courageously set about founding an old-age home in Colomiers, near Toulouse. Unfortunately our apartment was once again in an establishment that interfered with all privacy and intimacy.

By now we barely spoke to each other. Our silence was broken only by useless tantrums, cruel and awkward fights, in which neither of us got the other to listen, much less understand his or her own viewpoint. Our marriage was over. I was absentminded with everyone, no doubt impossible to live with, and no longer informed about anything. At the dinner table, drugged by my tranquilizers, I would sometimes burst into sobs or fall asleep in my chair in the middle of the meal. In spite of myself, I had become a bad father in every way. I had lost all hope of ever regaining the peace and calm of our early years together. As for my past, it continued to gnaw away at me. I felt lost, without a future.

In 1978, after a stormy return voyage from Brazil, where we had visited our son, who was a teacher, my wife emphatically told me that I was to leave our apartment: she had decided to file for divorce. It had nothing to do with my homosexuality. It was simply that our incompatibility had become blatant. And then, the image of decline that I presented was certainly unbearable for our children. A father's shame.

Thus it had been useless for me to endure what I had endured and to give up my homosexuality. It had been useless for me to spend thirty years building a home, because now my family was abandoning me.

My wife had bought a house near Toulouse. Family life, get-togethers during school vacations went on without me. I now saw my children only sporadically, during brief visits. The divorce case was going through the courts. Sometimes, when I dined with my wife, making vain

attempts at reconciliation, my throat cramped up, causing me atrocious pains.

Resigning myself, I found an extremely modest furnished room in the center of Toulouse. In the neighborhood, people whispered, "That's the man who weeps." I
had stopped taking tranquilizers. Instead, upon returning home after work, I didn't even wait to remove my hat
and coat; I simply pulled out bottles of red wine from my
shopping bag and drank, standing up, until I collapsed.
This was no craving; it was a way of killing myself, slowly
but inexorably. It was a cross between stubbornness and
disgust. I was unable to resist anything.

My shame, made up of a thousand other shames,
including what I had done to my family, pulled me down
in a dizzying spiral. I became fascinated with bums and
beggars. Every chance I got, I would ask them how they
managed to live in their condition. I wanted to persuade
myself that their lives, though precarious, were serene,
free of all constraint and concerns about social image.
Testing myself, I slept outdoors on a bench three times.

One winter evening in 1979, as I was wandering
through the utterly deserted streets of Toulouse, I
noticed a young man sleeping on a bench. The snow was
beginning to cover him dangerously. I shook him: "You
can't stay there!" It was close to Christmas. With no ulterior motive, I spontaneously decided to put him up. The
next day, my wife, who, aware of my distress, was coming
by regularly with clean linen, realized that someone else

was there, someone who smelled horrible. I told her I had taken in a homeless person. "Feed him well!" she replied supportively before quickly turning on her heel.

He was the unloved son of a baker whose wife and sister had accused the boy of stealing from the till. His father had brutally kicked him out. I tried in vain to intercede with them on his behalf. They all kept yelling, "We don't want to hear another word about him! He's a thief! Watch out!"

I let him have the key to my place for a long time. Today he's doing well, he's married, works in a restaurant, and calls me now and then to find out how I'm getting on.

One evening, one of my sons dropped by as I was drinking on my feet. He poured my bottle of Bordeaux down the sink and swore he would never see me again unless I mustered the courage to stop drinking. I understood his warning and tried to contain my suicidal despair.

I joined an association for psychological rehabilitation, where we painted, tinkered, and put on plays. The crucial aspect was the group dinners and discussions that followed these activities. I found some of their discussions beneficial. But I felt I was on the brink of an abyss. Today I am convinced that it wouldn't have taken much to push me over the edge.

One day I had a foretaste of insanity. I had been operated on for a benign lesion. But then they misread my doctor's orders. Confusing the similar-sounding names

of two hospitals, they decided that my week of convales-
cence should take place at a psychiatric institute. When I
arrived, I was told to hand my belt, shoelaces, and sus-
penders to an orderly. I saw that the window in my room
had solid bars. We ate across from an orderly, who
watched us carefully. We had no knives or forks, only
spoons. Terrified, haunted by my earlier nightmares, I
began to think that they were trying to keep me locked
up. I refused to eat. I tried to get access to a telephone. A
nurse ran after me to talk me out of it. They wanted to
give me tranquilizers, to calm me down. Luckily I managed to talk sense into the director of the clinic. He
allowed me to call my lawyer, then apologized for the
blunder and returned my belongings to me. My family
could finally pick me up. I had skirted madness.

Chapter 5
Out of the Closet: A Painful Testimony

On May 27, 1981, a week after François Mitterand became president of the French Republic, a debate was organized at a bookshop, Les Ombres blanches, on the rue Gambetta in Toulouse. The main topic was the Nazi deportations of homosexuals. I don't remember how I learned about the meeting. In any case, I entered the small discussion room in the basement and sat down in the back row. This way, at the least stirring of anxiety, I could flee discreetly. I was fifty-eight years old. I had been working at an insurance company since January 1969. I was making a final attempt at reconciliation with my wife and so I didn't want to stand out.

Jean-Pierre Joecker, the founder and publisher of *Masques*, a homosexual magazine, and his colleague Jean-Marie Combettes presented the most recent book put out by their new publishing house: *The Men with the Pink*

Triangles. This was the journal of an Austrian homosexual named Hans Heger, whom the Nazis had shipped off to a concentration camp. His testimony had already appeared in Germany, and excerpts were published two years later in the first issue of the French monthly *Gai Pied.*

Jean-Pierre Joecker presented his magazine, then the book. He described the deportation of German homosexuals and read several passages from that document. I shuddered. It had been forty years since I had last heard what I was hearing now. I found equivalent situations and descriptions of the same sufferings and the same savageries. My blocked memory was restored in bits and pieces. But no one seemed aware that similar things had happened in France. I wanted to shout from the back of the room: "I experienced the very same things!" But there was no question of my doing it. I held on to my anonymity.

I listened to the entire lecture and its epilogue. Then numerous people gathered around the speakers for more personal discussions. I silently waited my turn. I was anxious to speak to them. Then I said to Jean-Pierre Joecker:

"Monsieur, I myself went through the things you've been telling us about."

He jumped. "In the same camp?"

"No, in France. In the Alsatian camp at Schirmeck."

"But we've been searching for a long time, and we haven't found a single surviving witness of the homosexual deportations in Alsace!"

"Listen, don't misunderstand: I'm employed and I insist on remaining anonymous."

"I won't let go of you."

"But we can talk."

"You have to bear witness. Anonymously, if you wish. That's no problem. The main thing is to talk. You're carrying a very heavy secret, and it concerns a lot of people who died."

I felt I was suffocating in this basement. But at the same time I told myself with an incredible ferocity: "At last—it's out!" Then we exchanged addresses and agreed to meet the following day, after work, at Le Cristal, a bar on the boulevard de Strasbourg.

The next evening, we showed up punctually. For the first time in the more than thirty years since my mother's death, I could talk, which surprised me. The questions prodded my memory. I spoke slowly, terribly afraid to disclose my recollections. But there was one thing for which I was unable to find words: my rape by the Nazis at Gestapo headquarters.

When Jean-Pierre Joecker came to see me two months later, he brought a tape recorder. The interview appeared in a special issue of his magazine, which focused on *Bent*, a play inspired by Heger's book. Twelve years later, not a word of that interview has to be changed. Joecker wrote the introduction and conclusion of that anonymous dialogue, and his words hit home. He showed great sensitivity in drawing out the testimony that I carried within me.

And I still maintain my devout gratitude to him, even now that he is gone: both he and Jean-Marie Combettes died of AIDS.

That interview was the real start of everything that has happened. I realized we had a fight on our hands. Bear witness—I had to bear witness even if I did it anonymously. Was I the only one? I wanted to find out, track down other witnesses, for someone who shouts alone is easily suspect. And that suspicion hurts.

It is true that homosexual life had changed greatly during the preceding few years. A feverish solidarity led to film festivals, demonstrations with uncovered faces. The corner newsstand now carried the latest homosexual periodicals. Two generations had passed. The first, mine, had pretended to remember nothing at the Liberation. The Association Arcadie, which represented that generation, had displayed good manners, and that was all. The majority of its members were married and Catholic. Attacking their failure to change the situation of homosexuals in France, the following generation, that of 1968, was a lot ruder; it developed a network of solidarity and a more radical political discourse, assisted by the emergence of new venues. But all that upheaval concerned only the new generation. I myself had known nothing but bushes and secrecy.

My physical appearance now went against me in my encounters. I found myself reduced to complicated makeshift affairs with young, rootless men plagued by deep social and psychological problems. Do I carry like a scar the persistent dream of resuming my adolescent love? Of starting all over again on the day when history abandoned me? Of rediscovering those rare moments in 1940, when Jo and I embraced behind the rolls of cloth at the warehouse? Perhaps. But how can I wipe away the memory that still makes me cry out in my sleep some nights: the image of his murder by the Nazis?

A year passed. For a while, I frequented David and Jonathan, a warm homosexual group in Toulouse — one of the few enabling the young and not so young to meet in a convivial atmosphere. I spoke to them about hell: the earlier one, the hell of the Nazis and deportation.

Finally, one evening, the anonymity that I still tried to maintain literally exploded. The evening was sad, like so many others. I learned from my transistor radio that at the very last moment the bishop of Strasbourg had canceled all the reservations for rooms in his Catholic dormitory, which was to house participants in a meeting of European homosexuals organized in the European capital by ILGA, the international homosexual league. Some hundred participants thus found themselves in the streets on the eve of the convention. However, they could still hold their convention, thanks to Prime Minister Pierre Mauroy and Defense Minister Charles Hernu, who let them use a military encampment in a neighboring area.

During a press conference on that April 8, 1982, the bishop was asked why he had ordered that stunning cancellation. His response was categorical: "I consider homosexuality a sickness. I respect homosexuals just as I respect sick people. But if they wish to transform their sickness into health, I cannot agree." The media made a big fuss about this matter, and some militant homosexuals went to court.

Upon hearing the statements made by that bishop on my native soil, I sat up in bed. I was frightened, terrorized, outraged. Homosexuals sick? I had to react. I was seething with anger. I had to stop those words forever. And to do so, I had to bear witness, tell everything, demand restitution for my past, a past I shared with so many others, with people who had been buried and forgotten in Europe's darkest hours. I had to bear witness in order to protect the future, bear witness in order to overcome the amnesia of my contemporaries. Destroy my anonymity once and for all: write an open letter to Monsignor Elchinger, the bishop of Strasbourg.

I know how angry I can get. I didn't want to indulge in blind rage. For six months I drafted and redrafted that letter. The final version was ready on November 18, 1982. First I sent copies to everyone in my family. I had already notified them that I was preparing the text. I mailed the letter to the bishop as well as to the media and the homosexual press. My open letter was published in *Gai Pied* at the start of the bishop's trial in Strasbourg, where Jean-

Paul Aron, Renaud Camus, and numerous other homosexuals came to testify.

That day, the "defendant Léon Arthur Elchinger" was
represented by his lawyer. Like the district attorney, his
lawyer claimed that all these charges were inadmissible.
The court ruled in their favor: "The reported statements
were not directed at anyone mentioned by name or iden-
tifiable by name." Would the court have done the same if
the statements had been anti-Semitic? But the law does
not proceed against homophobia. The plaintiffs, who
were trying to change French legislation on that point,
appealed the verdict. In vain, for in the end the court
ordered them to pay a fine of 3o,ooo francs [about
$4,5oo] for defaming the bishop. And their final appeal to
the European Court proved fruitless.

Though my open letter to the bishop had little if any
resonance, I felt I had been released from a burdensome
secret. I now decided to begin a series of steps to have
the government recognize my deportation and thereby
the Nazi deportation of other homosexuals. My efforts
have been exhausting, and so far they have not been hon-
ored with any tangible results. I have had to overcome
ignorance—worse, incredulity, the full scope of which
I've experienced only now. I remember the young woman
who, sitting behind her desk, stopped recording my
information when I added the word *homosexual* to *deportee:* she gaped at me, flabbergasted. I asked her to continue taking my information. She abruptly jumped up

and called her superior. Did she think I was crazy? Or pulling her leg? My deportation file no longer existed: the word *homosexual* had been pronounced, nullifying the deportation itself. What she failed to understand in her naïveté was that this was exactly what I had experienced.

Those first few steps were very difficult, but once my wife learned the reason for my deportation, now publicly revealed, she decided on her own to suspend her divorce proceedings. She felt that my deportation and my homosexuality had nothing to do with her case. "A simple separation of property and of bed and board would be enough," she explained. "That way you can have complete independence in doing whatever you have to for your file." As for my employers, they had no objections to my having gone public. Once the trial was over, Monsignor Elchinger acknowledged my testimony and even wrote me a very humane letter.

I admit I found all these things reassuring. I suddenly felt surrounded by new respect for my identity. And I viewed myself with a lot more dignity, no doubt because I now had an obligation: to obtain recognition for the deportation of homosexuals. But still, could I have confidence in the future? So far, after ten years, I have not yet received any reparations.

My political support was uncertain. Shortly after settling in Toulouse, I had wanted, as a worker, to have the backing of the General Confederation of Labor. The Communist Party wasn't very far away, and I became a member. I liked their speeches attacking the law of money. And the Soviets weren't my primary enemies. However, I had the unfortunate habit of keeping my tie on when I arrived at a cell meeting right after work. Only one other comrade did the same—a teacher with whom I had a real bond. Did our neckties offend the others? I don't really think so, but we were told that our place was not in the Communist Party. I sadly took cognizance of those words. But in all fairness I must describe what the General Confederation of Labor implemented in its radio series in Toulouse: they recently did a broadcast about my testimony. The quality was so fine that I can regard that program as my true aural testament.

The years passed. I continued sending parts of my file to many social and political figures. The expense of postage and telegrams cut deep into my meager pension. Then, in winter of 1987, Jean Boisson's *Les Triangles Roses* was published. I had several meetings with the media and the public. They proved to be more open than the authorities. The things I had to say were not always heard in high places. I also gave a talk at the Beaubourg [a cultural center in Paris, officially known as the Pompidou Center] on October 13, 1988; there was a full-page announcement in *Globe*, a monthly. At the Beaubourg, the library was packed, and one of my sons was present. Both my wife and my children knew that I would not stop speaking out. Nevertheless, like my family in Alsace, they did not oppose my actions.

On February 9, 1989, I was interviewed on television by Frédéric Mitterrand. The telecast was preceded by major articles in *Télé 7 Jours* and *La Dépêche du Midi*. Coping with my public image on a mass scale was terrifying, but I submitted to the ordeal, for my file was dragging along ministerial corridors, and my letters remained unanswered. Furthermore it was very difficult tracking down the official documents about my deportation and getting them accepted by the proper authorities.

After that exhausting telecast, I returned home via Lourdes. I have always been fascinated by the cult of the Virgin Mary. It's like a silent adoration, a quest for timeless serenity. Is my fascination the vestige of a faith? Of a still inexpressible love? My love for my mother? In any case, it comes from very far away. Why is it that after some great ordeal my eyes always turn toward Lourdes, just as they turned toward that Virgin on a mountainside, that Virgin whom I could see above the Schirmeck camp on a clear day. As I have said, other inmates gazed wordlessly in the same direction, trying to make out her beloved silhouette. Why was it, when I reached a certain Polish church with the Russians, I buried the statue of the Virgin to protect her from vandals and bombings? I do not visit Lourdes to pray, for I no longer pray. All I do is greet Mary discreetly. I don't know what my respect and devotion are made of. But they channel my anxieties and protect both my integrity and my identity.

After being thrown out of the Communist Party, I soon realized that a political discourse was developing around the excluded and minorities. I was drawn to the association known as SOS Racisme. I made inquiries and started attending their meetings. One of its founders in Toulouse was the grandson of a famous Resistance fighter in that city. I liked these young rebels, who refused to put up with the oppression of minorities, rejected life in sordid industrial suburbs, and warded off the temptation of drugs, which are so complaisantly rampant in that life.

At one meeting in the hall of SOS Racisme, I finally stood up and described my experiences under Nazism, my deportation for homosexuality. I also pointed out the ingratitude of history, which erases anything that does not suit it officially. Moved and exhausted, I sat down. Everyone applauded. They decided to send us to Alsace. The trip was organized and financed by the Socialist Party of Haute-Garonne.

We went to Alsace on April 9, 1989, and were put up at the castle of Sélestat, transformed into a vast youth hostel in the middle of a magnificent and sprawling park. The Strasbourg city hall welcomed us with cocktails. I was able to hand over my file to her honor, the mayor. Then we visited the European Parliament, where the elected representatives explained the mandates and workings of their Chamber of Deputies. Finally we rode out to the Nazi concentration camps at Schirmeck and Struthof, a few miles west of Strasbourg.

At Schirmeck on that April 11, 1989, I could tell them almost nothing, for nothing was left: there were no barracks, no barbed wire, no observation towers, no gallows. Everything had been destroyed. The concentration camp had been replaced by small, pretty, flowery villas—the happy products of a municipal transformation of the terrain. I could never shut my eyes in any of them. The sole vestige of the camp is the cast-iron gate, which now "decorates" the entrance to the town hall. On its side, a plaque commemorates the Nazi carnage. At the exit from the train station, a monument shows an inmate caught by a dog at the arrival of a convoy; the image was put up to refresh the memories of those who have forgotten.

The reality of what had occurred in that place was hypocritically transformed into a symbolic plaque and sculpture; yet we are still haunted by the memory of that closed space. As for the "party room," that operatic pastiche where Karl Buck yelled out his hateful and grandiloquent speeches, it was recently torn down. Why? It too should have been preserved, for no one who heard that voice can forget where it all happened—right above the torture chambers. Karl Buck, hopping into his black car to escape advancing troops, was eventually caught. But after some botched trials, he was able to retire peacefully to his luxurious property in Rudesberg, near Stuttgart; he died twenty-two years later, in June 1977, at the age of eighty.

There was no trace of any of this. Upon returning to Toulouse, I decided to pen a few reflections about these methods of dodging collective memory. I sent a letter to the office of the president of the Republic, but received no acknowledgment of that letter and its contents until three years later.

At the Struthof camp, whose commandant was convicted at the Nuremberg Trial, things are better "preserved." A space remains, allowing reflection: a few barracks, an exhibition, and the crematorium, whose chimney reddened the long nights in the valley after days of butchery. Yet there are people who regularly try to burn down the wooden barracks in order to wipe out history.

Two women helped me cross the threshold of the camp at Struthof. I didn't appreciate their solicitous gesture, but I realized that if I hadn't been supported, I probably would have fallen. Getting hold of myself, I asked a guard whether the "pink triangles" had passed through this camp. He said yes. A few miles from there, I had worn a blue ribbon, but for the same reason.

Some members of our group felt sick during that visit. Indeed, despite their sober didacticism, those places emanate an unbearable horror. An obstinate, structured, scientifically regulated hatred of the masters for people who are weaker, "different." At the crematorium one person fainted. As for me, I was revisiting a familiar place, which, as a prisoner of the Nazis, I had helped to build, side by side with the dead, the tortured, the starving.

I asked to go off on my own, separating from the group in Mulhouse. The eldest participant by far, I was exhausted by the trip and filled with wrenching emotions. We said goodbye to one another warmly. Then I took the trolley and rented a hotel room. The following day, I went to pay my respects at the grave of my brother, the deputy-mayor, who had just died. Next I called up my other brothers and told them that my train would be leaving in a few hours. They all came to hug me on the station platform. I was happy about that solidarity, that recognition.

However, recognition is still slight, and hardly official. My file is still tangled up in red tape at the Ministry of War Veterans and War Victims. As for the overall deportations of homosexuals, that fact is still vigorously contested: for several years now, some groups have been trying to honor these victims on World Deportation Day, but they are still rejected by the official cortege.

In 1989 serious incidents occurred in many cities at this commemoration of all victims of the Nazi barbarism. In Besançon, some of the people watching the ceremony shouted: "Throw the fags into the ovens! They ought to start the ovens again and put them in!" The wreath for the homosexual deportees was trampled, which aroused the indignation of many people. In Paris, at the tip of the Ile de la Cité, a deportation monument has been put up at the apse of the Cathedral of

Notre-Dame; at the request of the Reverend Father Riquet, a fence was placed around it to keep out undesirable tributes. The homosexual delegation is not permitted to lay its wreath until after the "official" ceremony. In Lille, in 1992, when the vice president of the region of Nord-Pas-de-Calais brought the wreath for the deported homosexuals, he was pushed back three times by the police.

The idea of remembering the Nazi deportation of homosexuals was consecrated only recently by the introduction of commemorative plaques or specific monuments—with the assent of municipalities and the help of fund drives. But all these things occur far from France: on the main squares of Bologna, Frankfurt, The Hague, and even Sydney, there is now a place, opposite the "official" monument, to remember the Nazi treatment of homosexuals. A plaque is displayed at the Mauthausen concentration camp—at the initiative of the homosexual group of Vienna. In the center of Amsterdam, a pink marble triangle, one of whose points indicates the nearby house of Anne Frank, descends gradually into a canal. I can imagine that some day a memorial will exist somewhere in France.

In July 1990, Mayor Jean-Marie Bockel of Mulhouse wrote a letter to André Méric, state secretary in charge of war veterans and war victims: what was his intention in regard to official recognition of the Nazi deportation of homosexuals—a deportation "that history has unjustly forgotten"? A response appeared three weeks later in the *Journal officiel:*

> The homosexual victims of deportation are, like all the deportees, entitled to reparations . . . There is no reason why a homosexual cannot benefit from the title of political deportee or that of political internee if he meets the conditions stipulated in articles L. 286 ff. of this code.

Thus all I would have to do now is take the necessary bureaucratic steps. But they seem to run into a dead end. For how can I, after fifty years, assemble all the documents required by "articles L. 286 ff.," as was done, without major difficulties, by the other deportees right after the Liberation? It was only two years ago that the Ministry of Justice gave me a document proving my transfer from the Mulhouse prison to the camp at Schirmeck. Yet for the authorities this document is insufficient.

In the last letter (dated June 23, 1993) that I received from the Ministry of War Veterans and War Victims, the ministerial secretary emphasized that the ad hoc commission was not definitively rejecting my request to be considered a "political detainee"; nevertheless I was asked to produce two affidavits by "eyewitnesses," indicating that I had spent at least ninety days in Schirmeck. Otherwise the status of political deportee, which was granted to other victims of the Nazis, could not be granted to me.

Stupefying bureaucracy! Fifty years later, in a street in Toulouse, somebody is supposed to stop me during my solitary evening stroll and exclaim: "Why, I remember you! You were in Schirmeck with me!" Whom should I contact? Trying to fulfill that requirement, I sent hundreds of letters to all the parishes on the Lower Rhine and also placed ads in the local Alsatian press. What else can I possibly do? Have the authorities forgotten that with our prison uniforms, our shaved heads, and our starved faces, we all looked alike and that we were not allowed to communicate with one another? Have they forgotten that most of the Schirmeck archives were burned during the advance of Leclerc's Second Armored Division and that the Gestapo archives went back across the Rhine several months after the Liberation and have never turned up again? Despite all that, I'm supposed to find two people who would suddenly recognize me fifty years later!

This administrative demand, a legal requirement, is straight out of a Kafka novel. And I must submit, no doubt. The affidavits signed by my brothers do not suffice for the authorities. So then whom should I get in touch with? I was one of the youngest at Schirmeck. Today I'm seventy years old. What octogenarian, what nonagenarian who survived and is still alive today will hear about my appeal and, fully assured, cry out, "I remember you!" To what quixotic red tape is my struggle ultimately tied?

When I am overcome with rage, I take my hat and coat and defiantly walk the streets. I picture myself strolling through cemeteries that do not exist, the resting places of all the dead who barely ruffle the consciences of the living. And I feel like screaming. When will I succeed in having my deportation recognized? When will I succeed in having the overall Nazi deportation of homosexuals recognized? In my apartment house and throughout my neighborhood, many people greet me, politely listen to my news, and inquire about the progress of my case. I'm grateful to them and I appreciate their support. But what can I say to them?

When I have finished wandering, I go home. Then I light the candle that permanently burns in my kitchen when I am alone. That frail flame is my memory of Jo.

Geheime Staatspolizei
Staatspolizeistelle III/2
Mülhausen
II D.

Mülhausen, den 10.5.41.

9

An den
Leiter der Strafanstalt
in
M ü l h a u s e n

Betrifft: Überführung von Sicherungshäftlingen
Vorgang : Ohne

Die nachfolgend aufgeführten Sicherungshäftlinge, die zur
Zeit noch in der Strafanstalt Mülhausen einsitzen, werden am
Dienstag, den 13.5.1941 in das Sicherungslager Vorbruck
überführt. Ich bitte die Häftlinge am Dienstag, den 13.5.1941,
um 6,30 Uhr zum Transport bereit halten zu wollen.

1.) Seel, Peter, geboren 16.8.1923,

Weitere 6 Häftlinge werden am Montag, den 12.5.41 zur
Bereitstellung für den gleichen Zeitpunkt fernmündlich mit-
geteilt.

I.A.

[signature]

Document sent to Pierre Seel by the French Ministry of Justice. Dated May 10, 1941, this Gestapo letter pinpoints the transfer of Pierre Seel from the Mulhouse Prison to the Schirmeck camp. The names of the other inmates were removed by the ministry.

6.November 1941.

Tgb. Nr. *11 06* /41./AV.

An die

Sicherheitspolizei

Einsatzkommando III/2

M u l h a u s e n

Betrifft : Entlassung von Sicherungshäftlinge

Vorgang : Dortiges Schreiben vom 5.11.1941 - IID.-Ko

Anlagen : Personalakten.

Nachstehend aufgeführte Sicherungshäftlingen
wurden am 6.November 1941 aus der Sicherungshaft entlassen.
Die hier angefallenen Akten lege ich bei.
- S e e l Peter, geboren am 17.8.1923 in Hagenau

Der Lagerkommandant

ϟϟ Hauptsturmführer

The last document found: Pierre Seel's release from the Schirmeck camp was on November 6, 1941; the document was signed by the commandant, Karl Buck.

Nazi Camps in Alsace (1940-1944)

Metz

Merlenbach

Bitsch

Haguenau ▲ ● Sulzbach

● Strasbourg

SCHIRMECK-VORBRÜCH

○

○

STRUTHOF-NATSWILLER

Colmar ●

Sennheim ●

● Ensisheim

Altkirch

○ Principal camps   ● Secondary camps   ▲ Gestapo prison

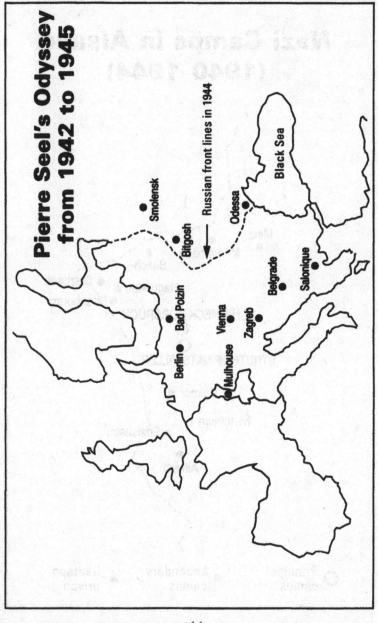

Pierre Seel's Odyssey from 1942 to 1945

Notes
By Jean Le Bitoux

Chapter 1:
An Average Middle-Class Family

10 "Homosexuality, by cutting the homosexual off from the bourgeoisie, enables him to see the blemishes of his class more sharply; it imposes a view of things more effectively than a political party does" (Andrè Malraux, quoted by Jean-Louis Bory in *Comment nous appelez-vous déjà?* [What Do You Call Us?], Calmann-Lévy, 1977, p. 132).

Chapter 2:
Schirmeck-Vorbrüch

15 Hitler became chancellor of Germany on January 20, 1933. He was forty-four years old. Two weeks

later he promulgated the law for "the protection of the nation." During the night of February 27–28, the Reichstag was set ablaze by Van der Lubbe, a young homosexual, who was probably manipulated. Hitler used the fire as a pretext for immediate suspension of all civil rights. On March 8, the first concentration camps were opened. Within two weeks, fifty camps were functioning. One year later, on June 30, 1934, the "Night of Long Knives," organized by Göring and Himmler, took place. Citing "homosexual debauchery," Hitler was thus able to get rid of the *Sturmabteilung* (SA) and its leader, Ernst Röhm.

The figure of Van der Lubbe was to be found at the origin of these manipulations. "In the Nazi press, Van der Lubbe, who set the Reichstag on fire, was the agent of a Bolshevik plot. In the eyes of the Communists and democrats, he was a confused homosexual. In fact, he was caught between propagandas, a condition that victimized homosexuals at that time. He was the negative hero of a history in which only the huge monsters of modern states confront one another. Crushed in the collision between Stalinism and Nazism, Van der Lubbe embodies our destiny: an incomprehensible victim without a lawyer, he was the harbinger of a massacre without reparations" (Guy Hocquenghem, *Gai Pied*, no. 1, April 1979).

17 "In 1870, the Alsatians had already witnessed the routing of an army that lost Alsace within two days; despite the strongest possible resistance, it was crushed by an enemy that was four times stronger because it had managed to concentrate in time" (Jean Ritter, *L'Alsace*, PUF, 1985).

18 "Coming two weeks after Pétain's announcement of the beneficial prospects opening up for France, the new politics of collaboration hit public opinion like an electric shock: inaugurated in Montoire, it led to the arrivals of priests, nuns, and families of peasants, who were supposed to implement the radical Germanization. The Germans forbade any mention of what was happening" (Rita Thalmann, *La Mise au pas, idéologie et stratégie sécuritaire dans la France occupée*, Fayard, 1991, p. 55).

18 "The mostly Catholic population of Alsace was kept on tenterhooks by the Reich's relentless mistreatment of religious institutions, which had been guaranteed protection for centuries whatever the alternations of regimes and governments and the specific maintenance of the area. The Germans declared at the very outset that they would not observe the 1801 concordat between Rome and France or extend to Alsace-Lorraine the 1933 concordat between Rome and Germany" (Thalmann, p. 62).

18 Regarding the amputations and divisions of French territory, see Thalmann.

19 "As of August 6, 1940, the Nazi Party chancellery ordered the removal of the French names of localities, streets, monuments, posters, and inscriptions throughout the three departments of Alsace-Lorraine. The use of French was outlawed in the schools" (Thalmann, p. 55).

19 "The only way to make the French understand the eviction of the Jews was to emphasize the priority of their right to work" (Thalmann, p. 146).

21 Camille Erreman, an Alsatian, was twenty-eight years old when he was arrested, interrogated, then expelled to the "free zone" in December 1940: "I had known since 1933 that the Germans were sending homosexuals to concentration camps: Alsatian friends had found out about it in Germany from homosexual friends, who lived in fear of being turned in. . . . I was arrested because my name was put on the French police list after a zealous judiciary proceeding, in which everyone was summoned to give his name. Certain queens came with their highly detailed address books and blabbed dangerously. In this way, hundreds of people were questioned between 1933 and 1937. The trial never took place. As for the commissioner of Colmar, who

handed over the lists, including this one, he kept his job throughout the war" (excerpts in *Gai Pied Hebdo*, no. 62, March 26, 1983).

22 The Nazi hatred of homosexuality was quite racial: "Homosexuality is a crime, not only against morality or religion, but against race" (Olga Wormser-Migot, *Le Système concentrationnaire* [Paris], 1968). This is confirmed by Jean Boisson: "The Jews were exterminated for being detrimental to the purity of the race, the homosexuals for being detrimental to the reproduction of the race" (*Le Triangle rose*, Robert Laffont, 1987, p. 51).

22 Heinrich Himmler said in a speech, February 18, 1937: "When we took power in 1933, we discovered the homosexual associations. They had 2 million members. This means that 7 or 8 percent of all men are homosexual. And if this does not change it will simply mean that our nation will be wiped out by this contagious disease. . . . If this vice continues spreading in Germany without our combating it, it will spell the end of Germany, the end of the Germanic world."

22 "The Third Reich proceeded to round up and arrest German and Alsatian homosexuals. . . . They were shipped off to concentration camps. The number of homosexual deportees is estimated at 350,000. Very

few of them survived. The victims have still not been recognized by official history" (Encyclopédie Hachette, 1990).

28 Aimé Spitz, an Alsatian and a famous member of the Resistance who was arrested by the Gestapo and sentenced to death by the German military tribunal, wrote an as yet unpublished memoir for the homosexual association David and Jonathan in which he points out: "The Gestapo's first objective in Alsace was to hunt down homosexuals. Its work was facilitated by the French police, which turned over the lists of Alsatian homosexuals. In this way, a good number were arrested and transferred to the camp at Schirmeck. Luckily I was not on the list" (excerpted in the magazine of that association, no. 3o, December 1980).

23 "We had no group or homosexual movement in Alsace, but we did form social groups in Strasbourg. To elude any surveillance, we met in a restaurant every Wednesday evening. . . . After one A.M., we would drive to an isolated café, whose owner was one of us. The password was: 'The doctors of Sélestat.' There we could rent rooms and we were free until morning" (Spitz).

24 "Anybody who is [homosexual] or even thinks of homosexual love is our enemy" (SS newspaper, May

14, 1928). As part of its virility cult, European Fascism persecuted homosexuals. In Mussolini's Italy, the "crime against race" included homosexuality. Many homosexuals were sent to penal colonies for years, especially on the island of San Dominio Tremini (see Ettore Scola's film *A Special Day*). These incarcerations are still not recognized by the Italian government (see the memoir of an Italian deportee in *Gai Pied Hebdo,* May 23, 1987).

25 A rare experience with a happy ending was reported by a German woman to Walter Kempowski (*Germans, Did You Know?*): "In 1936 I worked in a bookshop, where one of the employees was homosexual. They jailed him, planning to send him to Oranienburg [concentration camp]. One of my female friends then went to the Gestapo and made a fuss: 'Where is he? I can't live without him, my bed is desperately empty.' Ten days later, they released him—his head was completely shaved."

26 An internal document of the Mulhouse Gestapo, dated April 27, 1942, contains the statistics of the "preventive police action" between June 27, 1940, and that date. According to this document, 230 people, labeled "career criminals," pimps, and misfits, were evacuated to nonoccupied France, and 120 in the same category never returned from this evacuation, as well as 260 people in their entourage,

including those who did not return. Also evacuated were 95 homosexuals and 19 people in their entourage, 42 Gypsies and 240 people in their entourage. That same day, the German authorities also noted the presence of 33 "career criminals" and 9 homosexuals at the Schirmeck camp, 11 "career criminals" and one homosexual in security custody, 3 "career criminals," 91 prostitutes, and 154 "people unwilling to work, drunkards, and various misfits." Finally, "police surveillance" was planned for 227 "poachers" (*Homosexualität in der NS-Zeit,* Fischer, pp. 273–74).

We must nevertheless point out, as Richard Plant does, that in order to cover their tracks the Nazis used totally obscured and twisted administrative German in their notes and communiqués as well as their various orders. Thus, for a time, the German population confused *Konzentrationslager* (concentration camp) with *Konzertlager* (concert camp — a traditional place for music). This "confusion was nourished by the fact that people were led to believe that the prisoners played music and relaxed" (Kempowski, pp. 33 and 42).

27 The arrests of homosexuals discouraged the solidarity of the people around them, for homosexual friends were also threatened, as were their reticent families. In Germany, as Richard Plant notes in *The*

Pink Triangle (New York: Henry Holt, 1986) "homosexuals were generally deprived of all contact with the outside world; few families dared to admit having a son, a brother, a husband, or a relative interned for contravening Paragraph 175." (Paragraph 175 of the Prussian penal code defined homosexuality as a misdemeanor. The Nazis turned the misdemeanor into a crime with punishment ranging from forced labor to life imprisonment.)

28 Aimé Spitz (author of *Struthof, bagne nazi en France,* 1970), was secretary of the reception center at Lyons' exposition palace, which took in the expelled Alsatians. Spitz notes that 91 people were expelled for homosexuality between July 1, 1940, and the end of December 1940.

28 A letter from the German authorities, dated May 10, 1941, identifies Pierre Seel as being incarcerated at the prison of Mulhouse and specifies that he will be transferred to the camp at Schirmeck on May 13. This document was found in the archives of the prison of Mulhouse and was transmitted by the Minister of Justice, on December 24, 1985, to Seel; the covering letter from the assistant director stated: "After the investigations that I ordered in the German archives of the establishment, the only document that I have been able to unearth is this one, of which I am enclosing a photocopy."

A second letter, dated September 26, 1988, signed by the director of the penitentiary administration of the prisons of Mulhouse, and containing the same document, nevertheless indicates that "the investigations conducted in our archives have failed to pinpoint the date of the arrest or the cause [of Pierre Seel's presence in the Mulhouse prison]."

29 Numerous documents refer indiscriminately to Schirmeck, to Vorbrüch, or to Schirmeck-Vorbrüch. As for the neighboring camp in Struthof, it is also referred to as Natzwiller. Its commandant, Josef Kramer, unlike the commandant of Schirmeck, was sentenced to death at the Nuremberg Trial and executed (see Christian Bernadac, ed., *Les Médecins maudits,* France-Empire, 1967, p. 122).

30 In regard to the Gypsies in the neighboring camp at Struthof, see Jacques Héran's article about the "medical" experiments performed on them (*La Revue d'Alsace,* November 1990).

30 In this regard, see the excellent writings of Charles Bene, *L'Alsace dans les griffes nazies, organisations policières nazies, prisons et camps de déportation en Alsace,* vol. 5, dedicated to the memory of Aimé Spitz, as well as *De Struthof à la France libre,* Fetzer, Raon-l'Etape, Vosges, 1980.

32 Hans Heger, an Austrian pink triangle, recalled: "'The pink triangles, stay where you are!' That order was yelled out after roll call on a summer evening in June 1942. We stood in the deserted courtyard for a long time. . . . Then we were transferred to Sachsenhausen to work in the clinker-brick factory. We trembled, for that place was well-known. Within two months, which felt like years, only fifty of us were left. A final labor was inflicted on us before we left: we had to pile up some twenty corpses, which encrusted us with blood for a long time. . . . I saw a young, healthy pink triangle arrive. He was grabbed, molested, beaten, then thrown out into the cold for a whole night, then put under a shower, then alternately tied under a heat lamp and subjected to cold showers. He died very soon" (French translation excerpted in *Gai Pied*, no. 1, April 1979, p. 1).

35 As "degenerates" and "useless feeders," the mentally ill were likewise starved and massacred: some two hundred thousand in Germany and forty thousand in France during the Occupation. See Max Laffont, who studied what happened in a few French hospitals during that period: the Vinatier psychiatric hospital in Bron, near Lyon, and especially the one in Clermont, Oise, where injections, euthanasia, and malnutrition were the order of the day; the dreadful effects on the patients were

treated as credible research, and the reports were sent to the learned "Medical-Psychological Society" (Max Laffont, *L'Extermination douce*, AREFPPI, domain of Clermont, Le Cellier, 44850 Ligné). Also see Pierre Durand, *Le Train des fous*, Messidor, 1988.

Nor did psychiatrists and psychotherapists lag behind. The Psychoanalytic Society of Berlin, transformed into the Göring Institute after the marshal's cousin was appointed as its head, got to work without really turning a hair: "The members of the Göring Institute contributed to the German war effort. It formed a commission to 'cure' homosexuality and sterility having psychological causes; it collaborated with the labor front to prevent any revolt in the working class and it cooperated with the Ministry of War by doing psychological profiles that highlighted the enemy's weak points. Its study of France was based on a legacy of racial prejudices" (Roland Jaccard, *Le Monde*, May 13, 1987).

Finally, in regard to eugenics and euthanasia, see Benoît Massin's dossier in *La Recherche*, December 1990, Vol. 21. As for lobotomies, which consisted of burning parts of the brain to modify chiefly sexual behavior, they continued to be performed in Franco's prisons until the nineteen sixties by Dr. Moniz, chief physician of the prison of Madrid. The German inventor of the lobotomy in those black years was killed by one of his patients. Also see Yves

Navarre's, novel *Un Jardin d'acclimatation* (The Zoological Garden), which won the Prix Goncourt in 1980 (original French edition published by Flammarion).

37 Aimé Spitz: "In my labor unit, there was a young German with a pink triangle; he was twenty-seven and came from Düsseldorf. He often said to me, 'When we're liberated, I'd like to settle down with you.' One day an SS-man came for him and I never saw him again. In the death camps, you had to see everything, hear everything, but never say anything. That was how I survived" (*op. cit.*, written in June 1980 in Ingersheim).

38 "The homosexual is a man who is radically ill on a mental level. He is weak and acts cowardly in all decisive matters. The homosexual likewise lies in a sick way and believes what he says. The homosexual is by nature easily intimidated" (Heinrich Himmler, speech of February 18, 1937).

39 These excerpts from the memoirs of Jaroslav Bartl shed light on the situation of homosexuals at Buchenwald, Block 36: "We labored in the stone quarry under impossible conditions, constantly menaced by the rifles of the SS guards, the yells and blows of the overseers. Accidents and fatal injuries were par for the course, and no day passed

without the killing of one or more inmates. Almost every morning . . . the SS gave the Kapo a list of inmates who were not to come back. . . . One of the favorite sports of the overseers was to bludgeon the inmates when they were hauling the wagons. Within half an hour we had to lug them up one third of a mile, then hold on to them as they descended, for their own weight would have pulled them down at a considerable speed. If any wagon derailed, the one behind it would smash into the inmates, causing serious injuries. Often an inmate with a crushed leg was delivered to the infirmary. Once there, he was doomed: an SS doctor would give him a lethal injection" (Buchenwaldarchiv Sign. 31/27, quoted in *Homosexuelle Häftlinge im Konzentrationslager Buchenwald*, Nationale Mahn- und Gedenkstätte Buchenwald, 1987).

This memoir about the situation of homosexuals at Buchenwald is likewise drawn from the camp archives (*op. cit.*): "H. D., a commercial clerk, born in 1915, was arrested on March 20, 1938, for traveling to Prague illegally. . . . They had simultaneously arrested his intimate friend and extorted a confession from him. He was therefore sentenced to three and a half years in prison 'for indecent behavior.' After serving his time, he was sent to the concentration camp at Buchenwald. . . . Upon his arrival he was instantly confronted with the corpses of inmates of the disciplinary company, which were tossed in front of the entrance like sacks of grain. Moreover a young homosexual had hanged himself that evening, and everyone kept eating tranquilly without paying any attention. . . .

40 On January 4, 1942, H. D., a homosexual inmate of Buchenwald, "was sent to a medical laboratory, which was performing experiments with nettlerash fever, using chiefly young homosexuals as human guinea pigs. H. D. survived the disease but afterwards developed a heart condition. . . . Meanwhile the newly arrived homosexuals, condemned according to Paragraph 175, were quickly shot in the bunker" (*Homosexuelle Häftlinge im Konzentra-tionslager Buchenwald*, Nationale Mahn- und Gedenkstätte Buchenwald, 1987).

Other eyewitness accounts of medical "experiments" include this from another Buchenwald inmate, Eugen Kogon, who testified January 7, 1947 (quoted in the French edition of the British play by Martin Shermann, *Bent*): "Experiments were done by means of injections of medicaments, while operations performed on homosexuals ran a wide gamut. In many cases, synthetic glands were transplanted. I witnessed the deaths of two subjects of those experiments."

"The forced labor, the medical experiments, especially the efforts to burn living subjects in order to test phosphorous bombs, decimated the ranks of the homosexuals. According to the discipline of the third-level camps, homosexuals did not have the right to fall ill: they were not allowed to be admitted to the camp hospitals. Falling ill meant signing your death warrant" (Guy Hocquenghem, *Gai Pied,* no. 1, April 1979, p. 140).

"In 1943 Himmler decided to quite simply castrate homosexuals since they stubbornly refused to make the change demanded of them. . . . The authorities promised that every homosexual who let himself be castrated would soon be released for good behavior. . . . But when they left the camps, it was not to go home but to be sent into battle" (Jean Boisson, pp. 177–78).

At the Nuremberg Trial, Gebbart, the Nazi physician general, tried to exculpate himself: "Himmler could execute thousands of people with the stroke of a pen. . . . He told me that the experiments were expressly desired by the Führer, and the Führer's desire was a state order. I was bound by the SS oath" (quoted by Boisson, who adds, "But not by the Hippocratic oath").

41 "The great traumas of history have destinies that are distinctly identical with those affecting an individual. They are buried, the gaps are filled, but once

the memory pushes them aside, they remain as is, with the intact emotional charge associated with them" (Tony Lainé, preface to the French edition of George Eisen, *Children of the Holocaust*, Calmann-Lévy, 1993, p. 10).

42 "In 1944, I was in Danzig [Gdansk]. There was a shipyard. Women coming from Struthof marched three abreast. There were about a hundred, a hundred fifty, escorted by SS women in black uniforms; these guards wore boots and each one held a whip. And they drove those poor creatures" (memoir published in Walter Kempowski, p. 154).

Chapter 3:
Destination Smolensk

45 An example of how homosexuals were treated in the German concentration camps was cynically described by Rudolph Hösz, the head of a camp: "In Sachsenhausen, the homosexuals were all kept in a single barrack from the very outset. They worked, separated from the others, in a clay quarry. This hard work, meant to turn them normal, did not have the same influence on the diverse categories of homosexuals. While the men with a firm desire to renounce their habits showed that they were able to endure the harshest work, the rest slowly per-

ished. . . . Nor was it difficult to foresee a fatal out-come whenever one of those men lost his 'friend' to disease or death. . . . Many committed suicide. In some cases we saw a pair of friends killing one another simultaneously" (in *Le commandant d'Auschwitz parle*, Maspero).

The historian François Bédarida notes: "In the concentration camps, the Gypsies and homosexuals were at the bottom of the camp hierarchy. They were forced to do the most degrading and most arduous work. Thus a Gypsy woman whose entire family had been gassed was used to carry the dead. Together with other internees, she had to gather the corpses at the execution sites and carry them to the ditch, where the prisoners were often still alive, though barely. They were finished off with a bullet in the back of the neck" (*Politique nazie d'extermina-tion*, Institut d'histoire du temps présent, Albin Michel, p. 274).

46 The famous Chicago psychiatrist Bruno Bettel-heim, who, before War World II, was interned at Dachau, then Buchenwald, writes: "People survived not with a reduced self-respect but with none" (in *The Informed Heart*). "But it was a fact in the con-centration camps that those who had religious and moral convictions managed to survive better than the others" (*Survival and Other Essays*). Also see

Sylvie Graffard and Léo Tristan, *Les Bibelforscher et le nazisme* (Tirésias, 1990), about the deportations of thousands of Jehovah's Witnesses by the Third Reich.

52 "On August 9, 1942, during a meeting at Hitler's headquarters in the Ukraine, a decision was reached to introduce obligatory military service for the Alsatians and Lorrainers, who had shown little inclination to respond to the calls for volunteers" (Rita Thalmann, *La mise au pas, idéologie et stratégie sécuritaire dans la France occupée,* Fayard, 1991, p. 63). This was Hitler's revenge on the young Alsatians whom he had failed to win over: "Alsatians drafted by force into the Wehrmacht are fighting against their brothers. They are resented; anti-Alsatian racism. . . . Some flee from the German army, but reprisals against their families" (Cyril Collard, *L'Ange sauvage, carnets,* Flammarion, 1993, pp. 105–106).

During the German collapse, the entire population of the Alsatian village of Oradour-sur-Glane was massacred in its church. "At the trial after the Liberation, the only defendants present were Alsatians who had been forcibly conscripted; Alsace took it as a condemnation of all those unwilling draftees, whose first contingents had embarked against their will but while singing the

Marseillaise" (Jean Ritter, *L'Alsace,* PUF, 1985, p. 66). Of these hundred thousand draftees, less than half survived. As for the Alsatians who were condemned for committing the atrocity in that village, they were eventually pardoned by the French president.

53 After the assassination of Röhm and the rumors about homosexuality in the SA, Hitler, in his speech of November 11, 1936, raised his voice: "We have not hesitated to wipe out that plague with death, even in our own midst."

58 "It's useless for the administration to exalt the glorious mission of the new recruits, to throw parties in their honor; for very few draftees are willing to don the [German] uniform. Some try to get exempted because of tuberculosis or mental deficiency, some try to flee to Switzerland or the French interior, others hand out hostile leaflets or demonstrate during conscription sessions. In certain localities, the recruits are tipsy when they reach the barracks and they sing satirical ditties or even the Marseillaise, while holding up a French flag" (Thalmann, p. 63).

60 Rudolph Hösz, commandant of Sachsenhausen, then Auschwitz, wrote in his memoirs: "The homosexuals had to work day and night; few survived." Jean Danet, quoting Michel Foucault, writes that "this concentration camp is a cross between a hos-

pital and a farmyard. As sadistic experiments or disguised extermination, the medicalization of homosexuality finds its ultimate expression here, with a
dreadful irony. For a single blood-stained path runs
from Hirschfeld's theory of homosexuality to the
Soviet 'social peril' and Hitler's eugenics" (Hocquenghem, p. 141).

The British novelist Christopher Isherwood, who
was in Berlin during the dark years, writes in his
autobiographical *Christopher and His Kind:* "They
publicly burned the seized volumes and papers as
well as a bust of Hirschfeld on the opera square.
Christopher, present in the crowd, said, 'It's shameful!' but in a quiet voice."

In 1930, after twenty years of activism, Dr. Magnus
Hirschfeld, a Jew and a homosexual, started a peti-
tion, which ultimately bore 6,000 signatures,
including those of Lou Andreas Salomé and Rainer
Maria Rilke as well as three famous Nobel laureates:
Albert Einstein, Hermann Hesse, and Thomas
Mann. The goal was to abrogate Paragraph 175 of
the Prussian penal code, which for the past sixty
years had defined homosexuality as a misdemeanor,
an infraction against the social order. The Nazis
turned the misdemeanor into a crime punishable
with anything from ten years' forced labor to life
imprisonment. The Wehrmacht, especially after the
Night of Long Knives, likewise prohibited homo-

sexuality, sending the culprit directly into battle.

On May 15, 1935, Magnus Hirschfeld died of cardiac arrest in Nice. He is buried there, not far from Verdi, in the cemetery overlooking the sea. In 1920, he had suffered the first physical violence. In 1923, during a debate in Vienna, he was physically attacked. Next he lost his German citizenship. He was planning to move his institute to Nice.

As for Paragraph 175, it survived until 1979.

60   The nocturnal venues of homosexuals — bars, clubs, and parks — were emptied by a special unit of the national security forces; then the lists kept by the police and the courts did their job. More effective than anything else, denunciations thrived. Mere suspicion was enough. Thus vendettas brought an impressive harvest of people in more or less high places. On the basis of a hustler's perjury, for example, military headquarters was able to get rid of General Fitch, who defended himself valiantly against that "slander." This did not prevent him from being discharged or the hustler from being shot.

60   "I was denounced to the police by a friend who had been tortured until he revealed the name and address of every homosexual he knew. One day in fall 1934 — my concierge had just informed me down below — a policeman was waiting in my living room

to haul me off to Gestapo headquarters. It was after the assassination of Röhm, and the Nazis were hunting down homosexuals by raiding the gay bars and arrested everyone there. I was a famous actor. I kept shuttling between Columbia-Damm Prison and the Gestapo for interrogations. Then I was incarcerated in Lichtenburg Prison, which seemed to hold nothing but homosexuals. My life was saved only through the intervention of Heinz Hilpert, head of the Deutsches Theater in Berlin; he negotiated my release with Himmler by claiming that I was not homosexual, even though he knew perfectly well that I was" (Frank Rector, *The Nazi Extermination of Homosexuals*, Stein and Day, also published in the gay Canadian monthly *Le Berdache*, Montreal, September 1981).

61   See Marc Hillel, *Au Nom de la race*, Fayard, 1975.

61   "Gather a thousand girls. Force them to mate with a hundred young Germans. With a hundred camps of that kind, you will promptly create a pure-blooded generation of a hundred thousand children" (Dr. Willbard Hentschel in *Der Hammer*, a Nazi propaganda newspaper, vol. 640, p. 17). The Lebensborn centers, like the concentration camps, were the work of Heinrich Himmler, who committed suicide in 1945 with the collapse of Germany. It was he who said, "Those who practice homosexual-

ity deprive Germany of the children they owe her" (speech of January 26, 1938). He had only one obsession: pure blood and its forced reproduction: "I plan to seek German blood throughout the world. We will take everyone who is of good blood. . . . We will even steal their children and raise them here" (speech of November 8, 1938, and October 4, 1943, quoted by Jean Boisson, *Le Triangle rose*, Robert Laffont, 1987).

64 According to estimates by the Polish government, a hundred thousand blond Polish children were abducted by the Nazis (see the Warsaw daily, *Zicie Warozawy*, June 11, 1948). As for the Japanese army during World War II, while it did not compel kidnapped women to procreate, it did force thousands of Korean "comfort women" into prostitution for the troops. The Seoul government recently decided to compensate them, whereas the Japanese government, though acknowledging its responsibility, refuses to indemnify the 121 survivors who have been officially counted (*Le Monde*, September 2, 1993).

64 See Michel Tournier's novel *Le Roi des Aulnes* (The Ogre), Gallimard, 1970.

64 The two-page spread had a black background with captioned photographs of children ten years of age or older. The advertisement said, "Who can tell us

who we are, where we come from, when we were born? We thank you for any even minor detail concerning our origins. Please write to the German Red Cross." An example of one caption: "Search number 05170. Unknown. His name might be Jan Rominski, born in 1941 in Strasburg, Eastern Prussia. Jan is searching for his mother and further members of his family. His mother is probably Irena Rominska, who, in 1942, lived at 4 Lidzabarska Street in Brodninca."

67 One leaflet dropped over Berlin by Allied planes between two bombings of the Reich's capital read: "Terror. Terror was Hitler's weapon when he subjugated the German people and republic to serving his party. Terror was what Hitler used in Austria, Czechoslovakia, Poland, Norway, Belgium, Holland, France, Yugoslavia, and Greece. Terror against the civilian population. In the fall of 1940, against residential areas in order to bring Great Britain to its knees. Now Hitler is using the same weapons against Russia. But Hitler has grossly miscalculated. The war in Russia is continuing, and Great Britain is much stronger today than it was a year ago. And America is at its side. Now we are starting to respond to Hitler. And with bigger and bigger bombs. What you have experienced tonight are simply the first few drops announcing the storms to

come. Bombs will rain down upon Germany. That is how we are responding to Hitler. If this is too much for you, if you cannot endure this deluge, then make sure to thank Hitler for it. You owe this chaos to him. All your allies, even Hungary, Slovakia, and Rumania, are publishing the lists of their dead. But you Germans have no right to the truth."

79 "When the German concentration camps were opened in 1945, a wave of horror swept through Germany and the rest of the world. . . . Now among those victims there is one group that did not complain about what it had suffered and that found no understanding among the newspapers, administrations, or organizations defending the interests of the survivors: homosexuals. . . . They found no pity in the public and, naturally, could not claim any reparations. . . . In the camps, they were often given bad treatment. I myself once saw a slightly effeminate young man forced to dance in front of SS men, who then hanged him" (anonymous memoir published in *Rapport contre la normalité,* Champ Libre, 1971, p. 112).

88 "The chief obstacle after the Liberation was, of course, the refusal of all authorities to take the homosexual deportation into account. [Another obstacle was] the fear that induced the victims— and who can blame them?—to often hide the true

reasons for their deportation—namely, their homosexuality. After all, during the 1960s, such an admission could have led to further penal sanctions" (Guy Hocquenghem, *Race d'Ep,* Libre-Hallier, 1979, p. 137).

Chapter 4:
Years of Shame

89 "Alsace was not definitively liberated until March 1945. Strasbourg was reconquered under conditions made very precarious by the unforeseen recall of American troops, who were directed against the German offensive in the Ardennes" (Jean Ritter, *op. cit.,* p. 66).

91 "It is particularly shocking for me that upon my return from the camps I was considered a criminal and the worst sort of criminal to boot: a queer. I never tried to get reparations. For us queers there was no such thing, even though we had been sent to concentration camps without due process. It was a violation of our rights, a conduct unworthy of a constitutional state to unjustifiably tear a man away from his work, his family, his society, to imprison him, then to prevent him from recovering any rights, deprive him of the very right to be listened to and defend himself" (testimony in *Bent*).

91   "Understandably the few homosexuals lucky enough to escape the deliberate and murderous insanity of the Nazis remained torn in the depths of their souls, even after they regained freedom — a freedom that did not have the same scope as earlier, for they remained eternal prisoners of their calvary" (Jean Boisson, *op. cit.*, p. 200).

92   During his final interview, February 23, 1980, Jean-Paul Sartre was asked about the silence of intellectuals in regard to the decades of homosexual deportations:

"Why do your writings contain not a single word about the extermination of homosexuals by Stalin and Hitler?"

"I was unaware of those massacres, I didn't know that they were systematic or how many people were rounded up. I wasn't sure. The historians don't talk about it. I could reproach the dictators for a huge number of things, but I couldn't reproach them for this because I was ignorant about it" (Gilles Bardette, Claude Lochu, and Jean Le Bitoux, *Gai Pied,* March 1980).

92   "For a while, Admiral Darlan, second-in-command in Vichy, added to his other duties as head of government by taking over several ministries — Foreign Affairs, Navy, Information — and also the state secretariat of the Ministry of the Interior. In March 1941

he asked the prefects for 'lists' of Frenchmen incapable of 'national rectification'—especially members of outlawed parties and associations, func-
tionaries and agents of public organizations, cadres,
and persons of distinction" (Rita Thalmann, *La Mise
au pas, idéologie et stratégie sécuritaire dans la France
occupée,* Fayard, 1991, p. 259).

Admiral Darlan was pushed aside when Pierre
Laval returned. Darlan's official title as Marshal
Pétain's "dauphin" was seriously imperiled. But this
did not prevent him from sending Laval the following note on April 14, 1942: "My attention has been
drawn to a major homosexual scandal involving
sailors and civilians. . . . The only repressive measures currently in my power are disciplinary sanctions against the sailors. Current legislation does
not permit [me] to prosecute civilians. . . . The
impunity they are assured of encourages their activities. I therefore ask the Minister of Justice if it
would not be appropriate to envisage a procedure
and a law permitting [me] to go after civilians in the
same way."

The legal age for homosexual acts was to be
twenty-one, but only thirteen for heterosexual acts;
this was the first attempt at changing the Napoleonic Code, which had halted the prosecution of
"sodomites" a century and a half earlier, in 1792.
Three weeks later, May 8, 1942, a bill along those

lines was sent to the office of the head of state. And three months after that, Law no. 744 of August 6, 1942, published on August 27 in the *Journal officiel*, was signed by Pétain, Marshal of France, head of the French state, by Pierre Laval, the Minister of Justice and State Minister in the Ministry of Justice, by Joseph Barthélémy, State Minister in the Ministry of Justice, and by Abel Bonnard, ministerial secretary of state.

On Christmas Night 1942, Darlan was assassinated by a twenty-year-old man at the summer palace in Algiers; the reasons have never been elucidated (see Alexis Wassilieff, *Un Pavillion sans tache*, Grasset, 1986, as well as *Le Figaro*, December 24, 1986).

According to Michel Tournier: "Under the influence of the Germans, Vichy passed that law at the same time as the anti-Semitic laws. For the Nazis, Jews and homosexuals were one and the same. After the Liberation, the French right wing could have asked for nothing better than to keep both laws on the books. But the presence of the American army made it impossible to retain the anti-Semitic law. French rightists had to forgo them. . . . Nazism is defined essentially by its hatred of Jews and homosexuals. I became familiar with the subject when I wrote *Le Roi des Aulnes*. I read tons of documents both by and about the Nazis. . . . Furthermore, people always talk about the Jewish Holocaust, but never about the homosexual Holocaust. This censoring of a portion of the concentration-camp victims is bizarre. Eight hundred thousand people were massacred for being homosexual" (*Gai Pied,* no. 23, February 1981).

This law survived the Liberation, when the de Gaulle government cleansed the penal code of its collaborationist and anti-Semitic slag. Paragraph 3 of Article 331 punished homosexuality with prison terms of six months to three years. In 1962 the sanctions increased under de Gaulle's presidency: a homosexual misdemeanor earned twice the fine and prison term as a similar heterosexual misdemeanor. Homosexuality was called a "social scourge" like tuberculosis and alcoholism.

It was only under pressure from the media and homosexual organizations that François Mitterand declared: "Homosexuality must stop being a crime." Having been outlawed in 1942 by Marshal Pétain at Admiral Darlan's instigation, it was not decriminalized until August 4, 1982, by the French Parliament and Senate, at the behest of Robert Badinter, Minister of Justice, during Mitterand's first term of office. He told the Senate: "France must stop ignoring everything she owes to homosexuals."

92   On December 8, 1945, after the Liberation, Jean-Louis Bory received the Prix Goncourt for his novel *Mon Village à l'heure allemande* (My Village during the German Time). Later on, he wrote: "It is by crossing these repressive social fields, as if they were mine fields, that the homosexual who has acknowledged and recognized himself must maneuver his way in order to live as a homosexual—that is, to live period. These obstacles, which must be circumvented, climbed over, or toppled, define the borders of what the sociologists a bit pompously call 'the homosexual universe'" (Jean-Louis Bory, *op. cit.*, p. 88).

94   "The ultimate success of all these forms of oppression is self-oppression. It is reached when a homosexual has adopted and internalized the heterosexual conceptions of good and evil and keeps quiet for life" (Manifesto of the Homosexual Front of London, 1975).

Chapter 5:
Out of the Closet: A Painful Testimony

124 "Heger has broken his silence after more than thirty years. He finally dared to talk about his arrest as a young student in Vienna, his months in prison, and his incarceration in Sachsenhausen, then Flossen-

burg. His testimony confirms what happened to hundreds of thousands of victims of the Nazi regime who were put on the index by Paragraph 175. . . . His tale is not that of a hero, it is the Anne Frank anti-diary, the flip side of the legend of the camps, which allows us to understand the silent holocaust that engulfed the homosexual deportees, who are denied reparations even today. That may be what it means to be homosexual today: knowing that we are tied to a genocide for which no reparation is foreseen" (Guy Hocquenghem, preface to the French edition of Hans Heger, *Les Hommes au triangle rose, op. cit.,* 1981).

Inspired by this memoir of a homosexual in a concentration camp, Martin Shermann wrote the play *Bent,* which premiered in 1979 at London's Royal Court Theater. "Being a Jew and a homosexual, I felt it was essential to write a play about the tortures endured by both minorities," Shermann said. The play was then staged on Broadway, with Richard Gere in the lead. A French version, directed by Peter Chatel and starring Bruno Cremer, was mounted at the Théâtre de Paris on September 21, 1981. "One of the reasons behind the play was to make the public discover something that has remained hidden, like a stain. Almost as if the pink triangles tarnished the image of the camps. In a way, the persecution is continuing, everyone is pleased, and that is what is so pernicious," Shermann wrote. A screen adaptation with Richard Gere, to be directed by Costa-Gavras, has not come to fruition (*Bent*, text and appendixes).

125 "It is sometimes difficult to evoke memories, especially if a man has to plunge into the horror of the camps and if his most intimate life was broken at eighteen by absurd intolerance toward being different and by the arbitrariness of the police. We are now meeting a man of fifty-eight, in whom images of past and present collide with one another, in whom events blur and vanish, while suffering barely dissipates. A precarious, perhaps stammering backward look. And forty years later, he must keep enduring this dreadful, permanent menace, this collective forgetfulness, which forces him to testify anonymously. . . . His homecoming in Alsace was harsh, without contact, without company for many months. Later on, he married and left the area, but still haunted by his cruel memories of the camp, his arbitrary arrest, and this permanent injustice, for France still refuses to pay reparations to the deported homosexuals" (Jean-Pierre Joecker, introduction to the anonymous interview with Pierre Seel, reprinted in *Bent*, p. 138).

128 "Whether spoken in private or in public, such statements are destructive and they must be denounced

and fought no matter where, no matter what the circumstances. The moral authority attendant on a bishop's words reinforces the gravity [of this offense]. For many years now, I have been fighting against such words, such attitudes of shame, despair, and destruction. My writings are part of this struggle" (Dominique Fernandez, *Gai Pied Hebdo,* no. 47, December 11, 1982). This prelate's comments were even more shocking in that his job compels him to maintain a certain reserve. Indeed, "the French government still has the right—albeit a right that it has practically stopped exercising—to have a say in the naming of religious officials to whom it pays salaries; it was the government that appointed the bishop of Strasbourg, who also receives his canonical institution from the pope" (Jean Ritter, *L'Alsace,* PUF, 1985, p. 59).

128 Pierre Seel, open letter to Bishop Elchinger:
"I have decided to lend my fullest support to the numerous voices of all the men and women who feel offended by your statement of April 8, 1982. As a victim of Nazism, I publicly declare with all my strength that such statements have promoted and justified the extermination of millions of 'sick' people for political, religious, and racial reasons as well as for sexual behavior.

"I am not sick nor am I affected by any sickness.

I have no desire to return to the infirmaries where my homosexuality was treated—more precisely, a place located not far from the capital of Alsace. It was in 1941. I was only eighteen years old. I was arrested, tortured, beaten, imprisoned, interned beyond any due process, with no defense, no trial, no judgment.

"I am too worn out tonight to inform you of all the mental and physical tortures and the indescribable and unspeakable sufferings that I endured at that time. Since then I have lived my entire life with a terrible pain, which I have shared with my family since that arbitrary arrest.

"Your declaration of April 8, 1982, has aroused within me a swarm of atrocious memories, and I have decided at the age of fifty-nine to emerge from anonymity. Throughout my life, even today, I have never known hatred for anyone. And yet, suffering from the profound distress caused by that still present homophobia, I tremble at the thought of all the dead homosexuals and all those who, in this world, are, alas, still tortured and exterminated with so many other minorities." Dated November 18, 1982, this open letter was published in *Gai Pied Hebdo*, no. 47, December 11, 1982.

130 "Anti-Semitism is aimed at an other who is imperceptibly an other: it expresses the disquiet that the

non-Jew feels with this other who is almost indiscernible from the non-Jew, the malaise of the similar person facing the almost similar person. The distant proximity in which that person evolves, the person who is 'neither completely the same nor completely an other,' is the most dangerous border area, the area of the tension of passion par excellence; it is the area where brother nations and the worst enemies coexist. The Jew is the enemy brother. And that is the source of the ambivalent feelings he inspires: the Jew is different, but barely so, and he is resented twice as much for that misunderstanding" (Vladimir Jankélévitch, quoted by Gérard Bach Ignasse for the similarity of these reflections with the social status of homosexuals, in *Homosexuality: la reconnaissance?*, Espace Nuit, 1988, p. 60).

130 Bishop Elchinger's letter of February 22, 1992, to Pierre Seel:
"Dear Monsieur Pierre Seel,
"After my moving to a new home caused the dispersal of all my belongings, I have rediscovered your letter. . . . Please excuse me for replying at such a late date. I am also returning the documents, which may still be of use to you. With all my heart as a priest, I feel for the terrible sufferings that you have related. I am pained that because of misinfor-

mation (which was rectified by a court verdict in October 1984), you could believe that I despise homosexuals. In the past, many homosexuals have thanked me for the understanding and brotherly help that I have given them. I hope that your emotional and material situation has been regulated in the meantime. Being an old man in retirement, I am isolated and without the administrative connections that could be of assistance to you. I entrust your suffering and your disappointments to Him who understands us in our deepest depths and who esteems and loves us.

"Truly yours,
"Léon Arthur Elchinger"

131   In November 1987, Pierre Seel took a trip to Russia with the France-USSR Association. At the Kremlin, he wrote in the book of important guests: "Pierre Seel, homosexual deportee, arrested and tortured by the Nazis. My thanks to the Soviet Army and the Russian people." But he did not forget that in 1933 Stalin, several weeks before Hitler, began sending homosexuals to camps "for bourgeois decadence." Stalin's law was not rescinded until 1993, at the initiative of Boris Yeltsin.

132   On October 12, 1990, Pierre Seel also testified on Jean-Marie Cavada's program *La Marche du siècle* with Monsignor Gaillot, Jean Boisson, Roger

Stéphane, Geneviève Pastre, Dominique Fernandez, and Michaël Pollac. In the fall of 1990, Seel was likewise invited to Mâcon for a panel discussion on the deportations. The audience included numerous survivors of incarceration and members of the Resistance, including Monsieur and Madame Aubrac and the writer Sabine Zeitoun, author of *Ces enfants qu'il fallait sauver* (Those Children Who Had to Be Rescued) (Albin Michel, 1989). A panel discussion on "Resistance and Memory" was held in Lyon to mark the opening of the Museum of Resistance and Deportation; here Seel, through Yvan Levaï, reminded the audience of the forgotten deportation of homosexuals and he wrote in the museum's visitors' book: "For the homosexual deportees. Also for Charles and Roger Vendim, my young cousins, who were shot by the Nazis in Lyons."

Having testified for over ten years, Seel receives a lot of mail, including the three hundred letters that arrived after the broadcast of Daniel Mermet's two-day program about him, *Là-bas si j'y suis,* on April 14, 1993, on France Inter.

136 Pierre Vidal-Naquet: "I find it absolutely legitimate for homosexuals to recall the deportations of which they were victims. One of the great difficulties for the survivors is to write history objectively. . . . It is equally true that homosexuals were

the most despised group in the camps."

André Glucksmann: "If the hatred between different categories of inmates still exists, it proves that something remains of the totalitarian structure of the concentration camps" (*Gai Pied Hebdo,* May 11, 1985).

137 "As honorary president of the National Union of Deportees, I insist on pointing out that this fence was installed at our request," wrote the Reverend Father Riquet in *Le Figaro,* March 14, 1976.

137 "The municipality of The Hague has put up a monument that symbolizes the struggle against the oppression and persecution of homosexuals. This memorial, with a kind of blue ribbon at its base and a pink ribbon at its summit, is twenty-three feet high and unrolls in volutes. The Hague is the second Dutch city to put up a monument to gays. Since 1987, Amsterdam has had a triangular podium in pink marble in homage to homosexuals" (letter from Didier Estrade, *Gai-Pied,* October 1992).

138 "In rereading my manuscript, when it was too late to make revisions before printing, I realized I had forgotten a group of persecuted people: homosexuals" (Mull Harrid, *Science nazie, science de mort, l'extermination des juifs, des Tsiganes et des malades mentaux,* Odile Jacob, 1989). In regard to this standard

forgetfulness, see Michel Cressole, *Libération*, April 25, 1993.

138 Germany waited until 1988 to recognize the depor-tation of a single German homosexual. Then, at the initiative of the Greens and the SPD, the parlia-ment agreed to create a reparation fund for the "final" victims of the Nazis: homosexuals, Gypsies, people sterilized against their will, and the descen-dants of victims of euthanasia. See *Gay Infos*, August 1989, and *Gai Pied Hebdo*, May 16, 1987.

138 A document from the state secretary for deportees and war victims dated February 11, 1992, confirms that Pierre Seel was a person "doing forced labor in an enemy country, in enemy-occupied [non-French] territory, or in enemy-occupied French territory" between March 21, 1942, and September 26, 1942; the same document also confirmed that he was forced to serve in the German army from October 15, 1942, to August 7, 1945. For his sufferings and the perils he endured, Pierre Seel was recently indemnified by a check for, all told, 9,100 francs — about $1,300.

139 Letter from the Minister of War Veterans and War Victims, dated June 28, 1993, and received on July 2, mailed from Caen and signed Xavier Rouby of the Board of Statuses, Pensions, and Social Reintegration, Department of Statuses and Titles

(ref. no. 84606), a case followed by Madame S. Paparamborde, ref. no. 93.45.65.

Madame Paparamborde had previously written on May 5, 1993, that for lack of time the commission had been unable to examine this file during the national meeting on April 27, 1993. Then Jacques Coéffe, cabinet director, had indicated, in a letter dated June 23, 1993, that Pierre Seel would have to find two eyewitnesses "in order to establish the length of your internment."

139　New historical documents will soon be made available to historians thanks to Boris Yeltsin: four and a half miles of French archives that were seized by the Nazis in 1940. These archives from General Security and from the Ministry of the Interior were abandoned in a train in Czechoslovakia during the German retreat and then found by the Red Army. The existence of these documents was not revealed until 1991; in November 1992 Moscow decided to return them to France. See *Libération*, October 24, 1993.